INNER JIU JITSU

BECOME UNBREAKABLE, FOCUSED, AND READY TO WIN IN ANY SITUATION BY MASTERING YOUR INNER GAME

MARK GENCO

Foreword by
RIGAN MACHADO

Inner Jiu Jitsu:
Become Unbreakable, Focused, and Ready to Win
in any Situation by Mastering your Inner Game

For Maurizio

CONTENTS

FOREWORD

I HAVE BEEN PRACTICING my family's art of Jiu Jitsu all my life. It has benefitted me in innumerable ways physically as I learned how to use leverage in the most efficient way possible against my opponent. What I learned after years of practice is that the same principles I used physically on my opponents could be used in all aspects of life. The principles of leverage, using sensitivity, and controlling space are skills that will help anyone in both professional and personal arenas.

The author, Mark Genco, has created a book with the same mindset. He has been studying my particular style of Jiu-Jitsu for the past twelve years. Not only is he a practitioner of the physical side of the art, but he has also studied Eastern philosophy and religion, as well as the art of self-improvement. He adds a unique and much needed aspect to the art of Jiu Jitsu for the world.

Jiu Jitsu is not just an art on how to beat an opponent. Jiu Jitsu is an art that can better one's life. I feel this book will help anyone achieve more success in life.

—Rigan Machado
April 9, 2016

WHAT THIS BOOK
IS ABOUT

T HIS IS A book written for every type of Jiu Jitsu practitioner and human being who wants to succeed in life. Whether you are a die-hard competitor, a hobbyist with a family, a seasoned black belt, or a dabbling beginner, I guarantee you will find something of use in this book. In fact, the entire purpose of it is to make Jiu Jitsu useful for your daily life. The physical techniques and principles of Jiu Jitsu are such that they can be used by anyone, EVEN SOMEONE WHO DOESN'T TRAIN JIU JITSU. However, the underlying philosophy that supports the techniques are the perfect metaphors to enhance one's life, so being a practitioner of the art makes it easier to understand them. In fact, it can be said that true mastery of any martial art involves not just perfection of physical technique, but applying the art to one's life. This book will help you towards a more fulfilling path in martial arts and life mastery.

WHY SHOULD YOU READ THIS BOOK?

It is cliche to say that Jiu Jitsu will change your life. There are thousands upon thousands of testimonials from white belts to the highest ranked world champions that can state without any exaggeration that Jiu Jitsu made their lives better. Usually, it is stated that the practitioner was overweight, or did drugs, or was a criminal, or they were just living a life that was not as happy as it could be, but after doing Jiu Jitsu, everything changed.

If the problem was a physical one like being overweight, Jiu Jitsu helped them out because it is a physically demanding art.

Some practitioners were drug users and criminals prior to becoming involved with Jiu Jitsu. Jiu Jitsu can help people with this kind of past because the physicality of the art produces peak states and emotional changes within the body and brain. Certain behaviors and attitudes can get weeded out just by these key biochemical changes (like adrenaline, serotonin, and endorphin rushes.) Instead of being addicted to drugs, the practitioner gets addicted to a much more healthy subculture. (*One simple fact is that it's hard to practice Jiu Jitsu the next day when you're hung over . . .*)

Last but not least, it has been well-documented that something as simple as increased PHYSICAL health can lead to increased MENTAL health.

One does not need as dramatic a story as explained above however to benefit from the philosophy of Jiu Jitsu. Jiu Jitsu, like all martial arts, uses the body and mind in a beautiful way that personifies efficiency and sensitivity. This book seeks to extend the underlying concepts like this so that it seeps into every aspect of your life, making permanent positive change possible.

I know many Jiu Jitsu players who, although they are great athletes, **have yet to actualize their full human potential**. Maybe you know some as well. **Just because they have a gold medal or a black belt doesn't mean they are a black belt in the art of life**. *Some Jiu Jitsu players are terrible in their relationships, their finances, or their emotional control.* I know this book can help them because it's essentially a guide to applying these techniques to the parts of life that I have just described.

At the time of this writing, I am still teaching 6th Grade Social Studies. I love my job, but it hasn't paid well. However, thanks to some of the techniques I mention in this book, I am now doing better financially. I invest in stocks, have set up a financial plan for my future, and am essentially debt free.

In terms of my relationship with my wife, we have gone through some real wringers. I can't tell you the number of times when divorce nearly became a reality for us. However, I'm proud to say we are doing the work needed to make our relationship not just better, but **spectacular**.

This past summer, prior to the publication of this book, I really had to use these principles. My family and I had some awful events happen: (1) We suffered our first miscarriage, (2) my wife's physical and mental well-being were terrible, (3) we lost several family members, (4) I contracted viral meningitis, and (5) I completely tore my ACL and MCL in May of 2016 in which I received surgery for it in July two months later.

All of these things happened within 3 months of each other. To some people, the last item on that list might not seem like a big deal, but to me it was soul-crushing. Not being able to do Jiu Jitsu or even exercise brought me to my first state of depression. I lost my skill level, my strength, and my conditioning. I barely saw my Jiu Jitsu community. On top of that, my ulcerative colitis (a condition I've had since I was 21) slowed my healing down tremendously.

It was truly a dark time. Applying Jiu Jitsu on an Inner Level helped save my sanity. I am eternally grateful for it, and now I look at this period as a testing ground to apply Jiu Jitsu on my soul.

Before this time, I've been academically trained in Buddhist Studies and Comparative Religions. The university I went to was unique in that we were sometimes required to practice some of the techniques we studied from ancient traditions. The cool thing about that was, it sometimes worked!

Of course, it wasn't just from what I learned at the contemplative university I attended. I've been studying human development since I was 14, the same year I got serious about martial arts. My whole life has been about applying my Jiu-Jitsu training to all aspects of my life. Over time, I have come to realize the same thing that all great pioneers of martial arts have discovered before me: **The attributes and traits of perfecting a martial art can be the same ones that create a beautiful life**.

HOW TO USE
THIS BOOK

FRANKLY, YOU SHOULD use this book for every area of your life. If you are serious about success, then this book will help you succeed in life hands down. If you are a competitive Jiu Jitsu player, you can certainly use this book to help you attain your competition goals. However, I hope you will also use this book for things not related to Jiu Jitsu competition or practice.

Actually, you should experiment with that as soon as possible. Try applying the lessons in this book to something you never thought you would have, like a relationship, a job issue, or creating a life you desire. *You don't have to go through each chapter in order*. When you do read a chapter, finish it and try to apply the lesson. Have a notebook near you and write things down when the book tells you to! Be adventurous, be playful, and enjoy the ride. **If you are curious about possibility, you cannot and will not fail.**

Jiu Jitsu is a reflection of life. What happens on the mat, happens in life. If you use the same strategies to succeed on the mat, you will succeed in life.

THE MAIN PRINCIPLES

If you have practiced Jiu Jitsu even a little, you will notice certain key principles that keep popping up. I've chosen certain principles and turned them into metaphorical themes.

1. **Understanding and Mastering Space**
2. **Maximum efficiency**
3. **Changing the Angle**
4. **Using Leverage**
5. **Harnessing a good U.P.A. (Unified Plan of Action)**
6. **Sensitivity- This can mean the difference between a Black Belt or just a Blue Belt in life**

In the end, all of these physical principles will allow you to get the greater gift:

MENTAL, EMOTIONAL, AND SPIRITUAL IMPROVEMENT!

This last point cannot be emphasized enough. By doing the exercises in this book, you are guaranteed to achieve greater optimization of your life in ways you may not have done before. So congratulations! You are on the road to a greater life!

THE IMPORTANCE OF MEASURING PROGRESS

When I started to compete in Jiu Jitsu in a serious way, I took the advice of Erik Paulson and started to dissect my Jiu Jitsu game. I divided it into the following categories, then determined the areas where I needed the most improvement:

1. Guard

2. Bottom mount

3. Side Mount top

4. Side Mount bottom

5. Being in the Guard

6. Mount

7. Cardio

8. Strength

I also started to write down a journal of my Jiu Jitsu techniques. Eventually, I got Amechi's BJJ Journal App on iTunes, and that was a big help. I found that the computer was a great way to catalog and maintain knowledge of all the techniques I was learning, although sometimes I still used pencil and paper. The cool part of Amechi's journal App is twofold:

1. It allows you to remember and see your techniques at will.

2. It allows you look at when you practiced, who you beat, who you lost to, and keep notes on those experiences. I feel that is more important than the former. Journaling like this is essential for success. The moral of the story is: **If you want to progress, you have to be willing to make measurable tests for yourself. IF IT ISN'T MEASURABLE, IT'S NOT GOING TO BE EFFECTIVE.**[1]

---

1   Rothman, A. J., Gollwitzer, P. M., Grant, A. M., Neal, D. T., Sheeran, P., & Wood, W. (2015). Hale and Hearty Policies How Psychological Science Can Create and Maintain Healthy Habits. *Perspectives on Psychological*

Have you ever watched the NFL in the height of the Football season? Did you ever notice how much time is spent evaluating a sports team or particular player? They will take a team or player and DISSECT them in many different areas. They will rate the defensive team, the linemen, the offense, the passing game, the number of interceptions, the running game, the positive and negative attributes of the quarterback, the running back, etc. For each area, they will give a percentage to show a level of competence in all of the areas.

YOU NEED TO HAVE THIS TYPE OF MENTALITY. If you want success, you need to break down your life in a similar analytical fashion. You can divide it into an infinite amount of areas. However, let's keep it less than ten for now. Below I will present you with a generic list. (You can change it accordingly of course.) Put a number from 1-10 next to each area. Once you're done with that, turn those numbers into a pie chart like the one given so you can get an honest assessment of where you're at right now.

EVALUATE YOUR LIFE: RATE YOURSELF IN AT LEAST FIVE AREAS

1. PHYSICALLY

2. MENTALLY

3. EMOTIONALLY

4. SOCIALLY

5. FINANCIALLY

Science, 10(6), 701-705.

6. SPIRITUALITY

7. ORGANIZATION

8. FAMILY

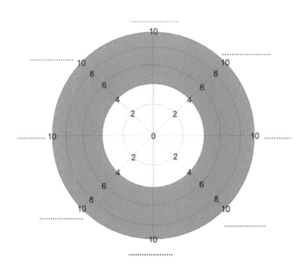

Unless you're superhuman and functioning perfectly in every realm of life, you might notice your "wheel" looks more like a partially eaten donut. Don't feel bad of course. In fact, you want to display this wheel where you can see it. Tape it to your mirror or to an area where you look at it every day. Constantly seeing this display will give you feedback on where you were and where you want to be.

One of the keys to success is constantly checking in with your goals. Make sure you do another wheel of life in two weeks and reevaluate. Use the techniques in this book to enact change in your life and test yourself again. Use the two-week rule over and over again and watch as your awareness and psychological toolbox grow.

As you use this book, your wheel of life will start to demonstrate more evenness and growth. It may never truly become 100% even, but it will become more balanced. However, the goal is not to make all parts of the wheel equal but to grow and become better than what you were previously. **Perfection may never be attained, but growth and progress are the ultimate goal!**

CHAPTER
1

BECOMING A MASTER
OF SPACE

Jiu Jitsu is the art of controlling space. By controlling the space between yourself and your opponent, you control the fight. In a physical confrontation or competition, space is defined as the DISTANCE between you and the other Jiu Jitsu player. Sometimes, we might not be talking about the distance between two distinct whole human bodies. Instead, we might mean the distance between your head and the pavement, or your head with a punch, or your leg with a kick. In this sense then, anyone from any martial art should be able to understand the connection we are about to explore. Jeet Kune Do, Kickboxing, and western boxing all take the various ranges seriously and address each range accordingly.

In this case, we see the classic scenario of a would-be attacker.

Figure 1: Notice the large amount of space. Space is a symbol of potentiality. At this stage, the space is so large that many things positive or negative could happen. With skill and training, you can take great advantage of this space and turn it into a positive!

Figure 2 If you lack those skills, however, the effects could be less than desirable.

You have most likely explored a scenario that starts like the above at your Jiu Jitsu gym hundreds of times. There is nothing too fancy about this physical situation. *But what is the deeper meaning to this?* How do we apply the same principles of this type of scenario to our life? Let's explore some possibilities:

In the Bhagavad Gita (a book you should definitely read if you haven't yet), there is an opening scene of Arjuna and Krsna (the key characters in this book) on the Field of Battle. Many interpret this field, not as a literal field, but a metaphorical field of awareness. Poor Arjuna sees a massive gathering of his cousins and other loved ones standing on the field before him, ready to fight his small army and close family members. He feels a great connection with them and feels terrible knowing they are there as his enemy.

Yet what does he do?

In the end, *he fights*.

This epic story has a lot to tell us about relationships. There's an aspect of your being that is distinctly YOU (Arjuna), and then a thing or person who is NOT you (all of his family members and mentors who he was willing to fight). You either engage with this person or object as a friend, foe, or neutral combatant.

Assuming you are dealing with this situation as one of an adversary, the first scenario is a common one in our life. You are just doing your business and suddenly, something or someone obstructs you, threatens you, interferes with your normal way of doing things, or does something that upsets you. How do we apply the same physical principles in a way that is not physical? This is the higher application of Jiu Jitsu, which I call *Inner Jiu Jitsu*.

**Large Amounts of Space is a Metaphor for
Large Amounts of Potential Change!**

Scenario one assumes a situation in which you still have a chance to take control in a powerful way. Let's assume an unwanted situation like the one shown above has occurred. Whether you like it or not, the complexity of life has revealed itself, and your space needs to be mastered by YOU.

To apply Inner Jiu Jitsu from a perspective of the first scenario then, please take a moment to recall a situation you did not like. It is imperative that you actually write down in detail what the situation was so you have every detail before you. Writing with pencil or pen is superior, although writing on a computer works as well.

You can certainly discuss the situation or altercation out loud, especially before you commence writing, but **you must avoid the tendency to just do this in your head**. To really get the greatest benefit, **YOU MUST DISCUSS, THEN WRITE IT DOWN**. By the way, since we're dealing with self-transformation, it's OK to talk out loud, especially if there is no one in the room. If there is someone in the room, then go find an empty room and feel free to talk it out loud before you start to write. We must not let petty and mundane ideas of embarrassment interfere with our self-improvement!

EXERCISE 1:

Think about a time in which you were not happy with how someone approached you. Perhaps it was an argument, an ugly comment, a bad look, or an unintended response that you were not anticipating. It could have come from a boss, a co-worker, your lover, a family member, a stranger, a friend, or anyone you can think of.

YOUR MISSION: Now you must apply the principles to scenario one. Our lives are structured in such a way that we MUST engage with others or with things outside ourselves. It is inevitable that we will encounter things and people in a way that is not aligned with our perceptions of how it *should* be. This will bring pain at times. In fact, it is one of the very definitions of pain and suffering. In one of the early canons of Pali Buddhism, the historical Buddha defines suffering as coming into contact with people or events you do not like or care for. Sometimes, ancient scripture can be so far removed from our human experience, but not in this case! How can we apply our principles of Inner Jiu Jitsu of Mastering Space in this case?

Principle 1 of Mastering Space:

YOU MUST ENGAGE. Recalling the beginning of the Bhagavad Gita we see a very despondent Arjuna who refuses to engage in battle. After some cajoling and insults(some playful, some not so playful), Krsna tears into Arjuna and gives him a truth. Despite the fact that Arjuna is faced with the terrible dilemma of fighting his own family, Krsna espouses him to get out of his despondency and FIGHT THE BATTLE.

This scene is something we should all be able to identify with. The field of battle (in case you haven't figured it out yet) is our life. Now we don't have to dramatize it so much as to say all life is a battle, but when you encounter someone who really gets under your skin, who hurts you with their words or their actions, even if they are a family member or loved one, the pain is intense. Now it is imperative then to take the first step. WE MUST ENGAGE.

Therefore, step 1 is about being relentless in your effort and intention to engage. You must want to engage, no matter the consequence. Notice, I didn't say you have to fight. You have to be willing to actually take action. Which particular action you should take will be discussed later, but right now, you have to focus on intensifying your mental energy to **DO SOMETHING**. Here's how:

1. If fear or laziness holds you back, here's a great way to start the process of ENGAGEMENT. Just like Scenario 1, where the attacker hasn't made contact yet, the first technique is less intimate and more psychological. Think about the pain you're feeling from not getting whatever it is you want. What is the specific pain you're associating with this issue or problem? WRITE down specifically what it is that you feel with this issue. I am assuming it's pain you associate with it, but be detailed. Be specific. What's the pain you might have associated with these actions in the past? For example, maybe in outer Jiu Jitsu, you kick ass, but when it comes to having a tough conversation with your mother, or girlfriend, or boss, you don't have the same results. Maybe you associate a really awkward, negative feeling with initiating that conversation. Maybe you become overly aggressive and lose your primary goal. Maybe you have a big plan that you haven't started and you associate the pain of losing precious time in sitting down and actually doing it. THINK, then WRITE.

2. Now, it can't all be pain, right? There must be some sort of pleasure or good feeling for not following through. Maybe the pleasure could be that instead of accomplishing that big project, you get more time to play video games, or you don't have to feel fear, or that awkward feeling from that tough conversation. Maybe if you hold off on spending money on a possible positive investment, the pleasure could be that you get to keep your money. Surely, there must be some sort of pleasure you're getting, no matter how small, that you can associate with this issue. Write down any pleasure that you are currently feeling or have felt in the past from not following through with what you want.

3. Now look at it from the opposite angle. What is the PAIN you think will happen if you DON'T follow through on your action? What will it cost you? Will you lose out on deepening your relationship with your spouse? Will you not be respected by your boss if you don't talk to him? Will you keep money in your bank account but miss out on a great opportunity by not investing? WRITE IT DOWN.

4. Finally, come back to some good feelings. What are all the positive emotions, benefits, and good feelings you could gain by following through? How will your life be enhanced by going for it? Really spend time listing all the positives here. You want your positives to outweigh the pain obviously. If the positives don't outweigh the negatives quantitatively, then they should overpower it on a qualitative level.

If you did this exercise, and really put your heart and soul in it, then you've taken your first step towards Mastering Your Space. Congratulations.

Example for using this Exercise

The first time I used this simple exercise was to get up super early for some Yoga classes that started at 5:30 A.M. These are the transcribed notes I took from my journal:

1. What is it that I want and what is the pain I associate with accomplishing this goal? *I want to get up early to engage in a consistent Yoga practice. The pain I associate with getting up early is the actual pain of feeling tired and groggy from not getting enough sleep. I also feel that I'll be grouchy and irritated*

all day from getting up so early. I hate the cold of the morning in winter and getting out of bed will be extra painful. Lastly, I won't be able to stay up as late the night before and that will make me even more irritated. The sense of being forced to sleep at an earlier hour will feel like my freedom will be infringed upon.

2. What is the pleasure of not attaining this goal? *If I don't force myself to get up early, I can literally sleep in more and get more minutes of much needed rest. I'll be able to stay up later the night before doing whatever it is I want. My sense of night freedom will remain intact and my overall emotions and body will feel slightly better because I'll be getting more sleep.*

3. What is the pain I will feel of not attaining this goal? *I will feel disappointed in myself for always talking about incorporating a daily Yoga routine but not actually living up to my word. Even though I will get some extra sleep, my body will not be getting the positive restorative effects of a daily Yoga routine and my overall athletic performance might suffer. In addition, I might be missing out on an important part of improving my Jiu Jitsu game. Without the healing effects of Yoga, I might be more prone to suffering an injury and that would cost me my larger goal of becoming better at Jiu Jitsu. I might actually inflict a huge wound in my overall training and my emotions and body will suffer tremendously. My ethic of discipline will be compromised and I won't be living from my highest self.*

4. What is the overall positive emotions and benefits I would gain from accomplishing this goal? *I feel that all aspects of my life would be enhanced from engaging in this practice. Yoga has*

a history of helping the physical dimensions of the body and I know my body could use those effects. All the hard training of Jiu Jitsu on the body through the week could be healed from this practice. This restoration of the body could truly enhance my athletic performance and overall being. Instead of feeling groggy through the day from losing sleep, I will probably feel more energized, alert, and happy from the mindfulness and optimizing physical postures. My work performance will be enhanced as I will be ready, washed, and prepared to go much earlier. I'll enjoy my commute to work more because I won't be in such a rush due to me being all prepared. In fact, I'll be more organized in general because I'll have to be ready the night before with all my stuff so I won't waste any time in the morning. I will completely be optimizing my time and energy in the best way possible! My metabolism will be increased early in the day and I won't have to necessarily feel like I have to work out in the evening. That means I'll have more time with my family! My wife and son will be happier and by virtue of them being happier, I'll be happier!

This simple example was an incredible game changer. As you see on the fourth part, my overall outcome of pleasure greatly exceeded the temporary negatives I would feel by waking up early. My overall life AND Jiu Jitsu became greatly enhanced through this one simple technique of writing out my pains and pleasures.

CHAPTER 2

CHANGE YOUR STATE, CHANGE YOUR SPACE

Figure 3: This scenario is a metaphor of life crushing you. Who better to embody that metaphor than the legend Rigan Machado demonstrating classic knee on belly control.

In the next case, the space was not dealt with while standing. As a result, the struggle has gone to the ground. The space is not so pronounced as the scenario we discussed in Mastering Space Part I. Instead of dealing with several feet of distance between one whole body to another, the space is now confined to a matter of 6-12 inches. Also, the overall openness is extremely limited because now the ground is playing an important factor.

The person on the bottom is in a precarious situation because he or she cannot withstand damage from punches AND the weight of gravity, along with the person's weight on top of them. How the defender responds and uses the space is extremely important. He has to take into account, not just the attacker, but also use the earth underneath in an intelligent way.

Basically, the distance between you and your partner is much closer, so therefore the game is different. You can say the stakes are higher. The opponent can now impose his or her will on you. Gravity and weight come into play here, and similarly, now the effects of not taking effective action can cause greater harm. From an outer Jiu Jitsu point of view, you're in deeper water!

In our second scenario, we need to carefully manipulate the space so that you are the one with the advantage. You probably have heard this at your gym. Control the space, and you control the fight. Here's a very easy and basic technique that demonstrates space control.

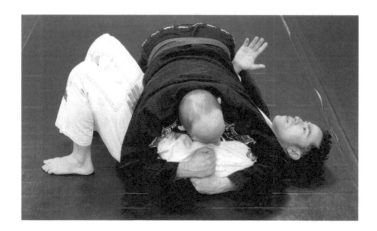

Figure 4: This position symbolizes how life can be completely smothering you.

Figure 5: But if you decide to change yourself instead of focusing on the things outside your influence, you can succeed. Notice the small amount of change created by the author on the bottom. His butt is only a couple inches off the ground.

Figure 6: Yet from the small changes we make, in this case, only a couple inches, a great sequence of positive change can open up for us. The same goes for life. Skillful and consistent changes, despite being small, will yield great success in our endeavors.

Figure 7: In this case, we attain the guard. The guard is the ultimate metaphor of although still being on the "bottom", we now have a great opportunity for success.

If you notice, in most of the techniques where the opponent is on the bottom, it is imperative that the person emphasizes his or her own space rather than try and manipulate the opponent's space. This is our entry into applying Inner Jiu Jitsu to our life again.

We can only do so much to influence another person or situation. Sometimes, life circumstances get completely out of our control. A person dies, a partner does or says something you had no idea she or he would. Our boss lays us off, or there is a huge delay in our project. Now what? We could try and talk our boss/partner/family member back into something more agreeable to us. They might change, but it is more likely that they will not. We have no control over other people. Certainly, we can influence them, but it can only go so far. As for life circumstances, sometimes we have NO control over them at all. In this case, we can only focus on ourselves. There is a well-known Tibetan Buddhist saying that fits this scenario: "*It is easier to put leather on the soles of one's feet than cover the world with leather.*"

Here are some ways to put "leather on your feet" so to speak. I have used these techniques and they are serious life changers. They will be for you too IF YOU ACTUALLY DO THEM CONSISTENTLY!!

Have I said that before? Are you doing the work? Do you believe in this possibility? Believe it my friend. Trust me. You aren't the only ones to use these techniques. Some of the very best men and women in the fields of finance, athletics, relationships, and life coaches use these techniques. Just try them wholeheartedly and I guarantee you will experience a SHIFT.

TECHNIQUE 1: GET IN A MORE POWERFUL STATE

Most of the time, when we want to change, it's because we are in a state of suffering. It sounds like a catch-22, but we have to get out of our suffering state first before we see change. Mahatma Gandhi said it best: "*Be the change you seek in the world.*" If you try to change while in a suffering painful state, then chances are you will not accomplish your goal, nor will you feel good in any way even attempting your goal, and frankly, the only thing you'll spread is more suffering. So **BE** awesome instead.

So this first technique is to help you change your emotional energy into a much more positive and energized level. You are mastering your psychology here, and hence your emotional mastery as well. Change comes much easier after you adjust your mind or emotions. Think about it: Your chances of performing better in a sport (whether it's Jiu Jitsu or otherwise) will increase if you actually FEEL awesome prior to performing it. You will be able to deliver so much easier if you feel better before making a project, or talking to the boss, or your wife or husband! So here we go!

DECIDE RIGHT NOW THAT YOU ARE GOING TO MOVE FOR AT LEAST 5 MINUTES FOR THIS TECHNIQUE!

This movement is crucial. It doesn't have to be grandiose or extremely hard like Crossfit (although it could); it can be as simple as swinging a light kettlebell, jumping up and down, burpees, dancing, or walking. In fact, I find walking very conducive to this. (If you want to keep this completely Jiu Jitsu oriented, do it while you're shrimping for a warm up.) It has to be some sort of physical exercise. Why? Because study after study after study conclusively proves that **exercise is the most surefire method to biochemically change the body in a way that makes you feel good**.

Although I hate drugs, the metaphor of drugs is the best because science proves that exercise is the closest thing to the "magic bullet" that so many people seek in drugs. Surely, you've already experienced this before, especially if you're a Jiu Jitsu player. How many times have you felt tired, lazy, cranky, or sore, and then you either forced yourself to exercise or someone dragged you into it and then afterward you were so amazed at your new attitude and state change that you were embarrassed by your previous feelings?

So choose your movement or exercise activity and then slow down after at least 3 minutes. Stop your activity for a moment and start to breathe.

There are two techniques that I will share with you now. In various Hatha Yoga lineages, there is a general rule of thumb of using your breath to alter your body and mind. Although there are many stages to this, we will be basic and short by keeping to this general rule: double the amount of exhaling to your inhaling. My general ratio is 4 to 8 with a 2-second pause in between.

Let's say you are walking. You start your walking vigorously for at least 3 minutes. Then stop walking entirely or go very slow until your breathing starts to normalize. After you relax to a comfortable state, start to intentionally inhale for 4 seconds, filling up your lungs comfortably to capacity, hold for 2 seconds, and then exhale completely for 8 seconds. I usually just count this in my head.

The good news is this: as long as you're getting close to doubling your exhale you're doing the technique right. You do not need to be so rigid about the exact count. As a Hatha Yoga teacher, I sometimes laugh at the strictness that people will go in their pranayama (breath control). Please relax and just do your best. Remember, the general rule is to at least double your exhalation. If you're gritting your teeth or furrowing your brows, you're trying too hard. This breathing phase is meant to relax you.

Now the next stage is a little different. As the body and mind start to relax and become more aligned with each other, you want to intentionally increase your body energy by pushing the breath. Start to very intentionally inhale for 2 distinct and separate inhales and 2 very separate exhales.

It is a little rapid, and you can play with the duration of the actual count if you need, but do it until you feel your body and mind change. It may only take 30 to 60 seconds to feel the change. Once that happens, amp it up to 3 breaths in, 3 breaths out. You can stay at 3 breaths in, 3 breaths out for the rest of this technique or you can move it to 4 breaths in, 4 breaths out. Decide on whether you like 3 or 4 better and stick with it for the remainder of this exercise.

Each time you exhale, there is a small muscular contraction of active and rapid exhalation. It is also more audible. If you are doing the 5-minute version of this movement/breathing stage, choose to do this style of breathing for at least 2 minutes then.

This breathing technique *is* simple, yes, but also a first step towards a huge game changer.

STATEMENT OF POWER

After doing the breathing technique for at least 3 minutes, it's crucial not to just stay in a physically altered state without involving the mind somehow. (Coming from a non-dual perspective, our minds are already becoming changed with the physical breathing, but we just want to focus on the mind aspect more with the next technique). If you're doing the quick 5-minute version of this, then after the first 3 minutes, you start to do a series of belief changing statements. These statements have to be personal to you. You can pick generic statements that have been done by others, but if you want real change, *create* a statement that is SPECIFIC TO YOUR MIND OR BODY AND TO YOUR CIRCUMSTANCE OR SITUATION.

Let's say you need to build more self-confidence. Maybe it's because there is a tough Jiu Jitsu player at the gym who you feel so inadequate against, or maybe it's a co-worker that makes you feel uneasy. Maybe it's just really bad family dynamics. Whatever it is, choose a statement that is somewhat general, but also specific for your life.

So let's say that it's confidence that you need to deal with all the aforementioned problems. Your statement of power should be something like, "ALL THE CONFIDENCE I NEED IS WITHIN ME NOW."

Take time to create several different Statements of Power for each of the feelings you need to overcome. Is it more confidence you need? More love? More joy? More money?? (While money isn't a feeling, it can certainly help with feeling strong and successful.) Decide on a couple different power statements and then WRITE THEM DOWN. Once written down, test them. Do they adequately and briefly express an attribute, skill, habit, or trait you desire?

Now, whether you are successful or not depends on two main points: HOW you say it, and HOW MUCH you say it. It really comes down to this.

So for example, let's say you decide on stating your truth as, "All the confidence I need is within me now" with little energy, or a feeling or nonchalance, it will do nothing. It will stay at the periphery of your consciousness. You have to penetrate the mind's bubbly superficialness and let the words become your STATEMENT OF POWER.

Now how do you do this? First, you start to believe or even just attempt to believe that YOU DO HAVE ALL THE CONFIDENCE YOU NEED. It can start as a spark, but you start to consider the possibility that all the confidence you need is actually within, waiting to be realized. You use your body in a way that also expresses the words. You don't just passively walk like you're going to buy some groceries, you let your imagination run and let the body express how it would feel to believe that you **HAVE ALL THE CONFIDENCE YOU NEED IN YOU RIGHT NOW AT THIS MOMENT, AT THIS TIME.** It should start to escalate and become fired up in your soul. Your face should express it, your speech and tone of your words should express the change, and the body language should feel it and express it. Your chest becomes more emboldened. You can actually feel the words emanating from your throat with the ring of pure, undiluted truth.

Once you start to experience the feeling of belief, or realness, of the possibility that you do indeed have all the confidence you need right now, it will take a life of its own. You can shout it out at the top of your lungs, or speak it with a sense of sacredness because it expresses a deep spiritual truth. You can change the rhythm and feeling of how you say it. You need to have fun with it so you enjoy it. It can even start comically, but eventually, you must say it with CERTAINTY. Once you achieve that feeling of certainty, you can turn it into whatever works for you.

Now it's time to test your STATEMENT OF POWER. First, try just thinking it. Think and say it in your head but not with your vocal cords. Does it feel right? It should. If it doesn't, then reformulate it so it does. It should be short, but be real and pertinent to you. Now don't overthink it either. This should be a general psychological attribute you're looking to gain more of. Once you've said it mentally to yourself and it feels good, go and venture to say it out loud. Feel it in your body and mind. Keep repeating it while you're exercising. If the statement has a rhythm that works with your exercise, you will be doubling your success.

Get into your statement and work towards the feeling of certainty. You chant your Statement of Power until it feels real to you and you keep chanting it for a period of time.

Sample Statements of Power

"All the Confidence I need is already INSIDE of me NOW"

"All the Certainty I need is already INSIDE of me NOW"

"All the Happiness I need is already INSIDE of me NOW"

"I AM THE POWER I SEEK"

"I AM THE CONFIDENCE I SEEK"

If you are a religious type, there are ways to meld this in with religious thinking. In Kashmir Shaivism[1], there is a powerful school of thought known as the teachings of *Matrika* or *Vac*. These scriputres refer to the power of language in creating reality.

Matrika is a word that translates to something like "little mothers". The idea is that the sounds of language are the creators or "mothers" of the universe. Vac is considered a goddess in Hinduism with similar attributes. There is a line in a powerful but mostly unknown text known as the *Pratyabhijna hrdayam*[2] (the Heart of Recognition text). There are 4 distinct "levels" so to speak. The first level deals with the metaphysical level and states that the universe is single and whole prior to any division imagined. The second deals with the first inkling of separation of thought from primordial consciousness. The third deals with the beginning of the consciousness of speech as we know it. This is a huge and crucial point of creation for us. We define our reality, whether we know it or accept it or not, by our speech. (By the way, if you want to really explore this powerful spirituality more fully, check out the work of my friend Chris Wallis[3] who is a scholar and practitioner of this kind of stuff).

---

1   A beautiful and eloquent Tantric System of Hinduism.

2   A seminal work of Kashmir Shavism from 1000 C.E. containing only 20 aphorisms but limitless wisdom.

3   www.tantrikstudies.org

Why does this appeal to us, and how can it help us? Basically, words and the meanings we ascribe to them influence and control our sense of reality. We are constantly creating universes of reality with words. We run through this 4-fold sequence that the sages of Tantra have articulated tens of thousands of times a day. Why is an orange an orange and not a bicycle? Because we have been taught to associate a certain meaning and interpretation to the sound of "o-r-a-n-g-e". Yes, the meaning and image of those pre-arranged sounds are fluid, but ultimately, we get a certain picture of reality when it relates to "orange-ness". This is how we ascribe meanings to all of our words. From our words, we start to develop a "reality" of the world made out of the meanings and interpretations we classify on all the particularities of existence. The question then becomes: How real is the reality behind our words?

The answer is simple: *As much reality as you give it.*

All the great truths of the world seem to run on some simple thoughts. However, just because they are simple doesn't mean we follow them too easy. Only when a thought is carried through to the next stage of belief does it become a trait for success or failure.

Think of all the times where we failed at something, not because of our lack of skills or preparation but because we simply did not believe in ourselves. In fact, you could argue that not believing in yourself and failing is actually not about not believing in ourselves but rather choosing to believe in a story that we are inadequate or not good enough.

Similarly, you can probably relate to a time when you chose not to believe in a certain narrative or story about your life in favor of a different set of words. When you did that, did you achieve success or failure? Even if you "failed" to achieve your outcome, the quality of the experience was probably much different and more positive than you initially thought.

Our words are extensions of our thoughts, and we create our reality from them. Consider the first lines of the Dhammapada[4]:

"We are what we think,
All that we are arises from our thoughts.
With our thoughts, we make the world."

This point is so simple, yet so true. Our thoughts can either bind us or free us. They are, in and of themselves, nothing. On a biological level, they are simply proteins crossing over a tenuous membrane. Yet, they have the ability to enslave us or send us to our highest successes.

Whether you believe in Power Statements or not, your belief or non-belief will be true according to your thoughts. Whether you believe you can or can't, either way, you're right.

Listen to the next line:

*"**Speak** or act with an impure mind*
and trouble will follow you
as the wheel follows the ox that draws the cart."

Don't we follow our Statements of Power already? Usually, they are statements of limitation and trivialness. So many times in my Jiu Jitsu career, I did not win a match because I had some awful statements I was listening to. These statements were tied to self-doubt and worry, and they caused me anxiety. I was left feeling inadequate.

---

4   A collection of sayings attributed to the Buddha. Byron, Thomas. Dhammapada, the Sayings of the Buddha. Shambhala: New York 1993.

Of course, when I competed, I did my best, but my thoughts held me back. In the end, I didn't feel as good as I should have, regardless of the outcome.

Now look at the follow-up verse of the Buddha and consider its value towards your own situation and to your Statement of Power in particular:

> *"We are what we think.*
> *All that we are arises with our thoughts.*
> *With our thoughts, we make the world.*
> ***Speak*** *or act with a pure mind*
> *And happiness will follow you*
> *As your shadow, unshakable."*

This is huge. In fact, it is literally life changing. The good news is: these six simple lines offer you the chance to change your life instantly. It is simple yet profound. To some people, it might seem hard to implement but it is difficult only to the degree that we don't follow it.

There have been so many instances in my life where I was following my thoughts for so long that they turned into beliefs. These beliefs shaped my life, and not always for the best. They caused so much unneeded suffering and pain.

Once I took the step of formulating positive Statements of Power, I changed my life around. Make no mistake though: it wasn't immediate. I struggled with the contrived nature of these statements at first. They felt silly, fake, and superficial. But then I realized that this was all just a thought, and thoughts can be changed. I can choose different thoughts and a different belief system.

Once I changed my beliefs, I changed my life. It was that quick and that simple. (It continues to happen on a moment to moment basis although I've definitely altered my baseline state.) This can happen to YOU at anytime, at any moment. It's like Vitruvius says in <u>Lego Movie</u>, "You just need to BELIEVE." Better yet, this idea is displayed perfectly with Chirrut Imwe in Star Wars: Rogue One. Believe in your Statement of Power, no matter how contrived it may sound. Go deep, form the Statement of Power that serves you, and then speak it loud, knowing that it emanates from the Core of your Being, which is an emanation of the Universe, and you are a Co-Creator of the Universe. Let that belief crush any limiting thought you may have on it.

This is the secret that all great successful men and women have lived by. This will make you a MASTER OF YOUR SPACE. By accomplishing this, you may change the circumstances of life to your favor. If you don't, you'll at least be in a space that feels way better than before because your state of mind will be better. Think of the following physical technique to see this metaphor clearly:

Figure 8: In this case, Rickson Gracie Black Belt Luiz Claudio is in a horrible position with his back taken. This is a metaphor of negative beliefs crushing us.

Figure 9: But with skillful application of thought changing statements, the practitioner can literally turn the tables in their life situations!

Figure 10: Now Rickson Gracie Black Belt Luiz Claudio is the one calling the shots! Power Statements have the power to transform your psychology, and therefore your outcomes in life.[5]

As you continue with your chanting of your Power Statements, you want to start to align them with specific intentions for your day and week. Fine tune your statements to things you would like to see happen for the day or week. While you are creating these statements, truly envision the precise outcome or effects you desire.

---

5   Luiz Claudio is a 4th degree black belt from the legend Rickson Gracie. He teaches UFC stars Juliana Pena, Ben Rothwell, and Ricardo Llamas amongst many others. Look him up at http://lcctbjjusa.com/

For example, you might start with a generalized Power Statement like, "All the confidence I seek is within me NOW." As you're chanting this in your car or on your walk, you then supplement it with a particular meeting with a client or boss where you are simply a giant of confidence. **You see yourself embodying the feeling of confidence within you and acting accordingly**. As you go through **visualizing** and chanting, you should **feel** your actual physical body start to change.

I find that the best time to do this is while I'm driving to work because I have a long commute. Although I miss out on the physical exercise mentioned before, I am able to really give it my all in terms of yelling and asserting with my voice in the car. I actually feel my back straighten and face smile as I chant because I literally am *becoming the change I am seeking*. After some practice, your body will not know the difference between the actual life events and the vision you are creating in your mind. That's the effect you want.

END THE PRACTICE WITH GRATEFULNESS

After several minutes of chanting your statements of power, you want to ease out of your chanting mindset so you can move on with your day. Much like when you exercise intensely, you don't want to abruptly STOP; you need a "cool down" phase. One of the best ways to slowly come out of the state of power is to let the statements go and start to think of things you are grateful for. If you are pressed for time, then think of just three things. Imagine not having or losing those things and cultivate a real sense of gratefulness. Then come back to the present and feel how wonderful it is to have those things.

Sometimes, I am angry because my car is not a Tesla. But then, I start to imagine myself without a car, relying on co-workers for a ride, or my wife constantly having to drive me everywhere. I imagine the inconvenience of it all and then come back to what I have, namely a car that works and takes me from A to B usually without too much interference. This practice erodes the neurotic tendency of wanting things to be "perfect" all the time.

When I finally got to practice Jiu Jitsu practice again after 7 months of not training due to my ACL knee surgery, I was filled with tons of anxiety and nervousness. After the first month back though, I started to deliberately practice a couple minutes of gratefulness right before Jiu Jitsu class. The results were amazing! I would contemplate that just months ago I could barely walk and now I was doing Jiu Jitsu again. My state changed so much it was palpable to all in the room. Even if the instructor wasn't teaching the coolest technique, the sparring was slightly stale, or the gym was inconveniently crowded, I was ecstatic; for I was practicing and moving again. Every little thing from the ability to put on my spats, to being able to shrimp was performed from the point of view of being born anew. I became grateful for everything I could see, touch, feel, and do. The coolest thing that continues to happen is that when I practice gratefulness, I roll better. My theory is that I put myself in an altered state of positive openness, which allows my body to respond in a more flow like state. Try it for yourself in any life endeavor and see what happens!

Quick Summary for Changing your State:

1. **Perform some sort of physical exercise or movement**
2. **Do the breathing exercise**

3. **Engage in your Power Statements**

4. **End with Gratefulness**

If you're pressed for time, create a session of 3 minutes each. If you have more time, go for 10 minutes each. You'll be buzzing by the end!

CHAPTER

3

SACRED SPACE, SACRED MIND

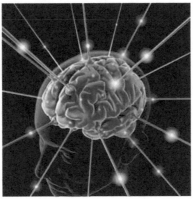

S O BY NOW, you should understand the divine principle of dealing with the personal Space of your mind. When you master the Space of your mind, you are undefeatable. To use the metaphor from before, the Space at this point is extremely sacred and important. If you don't handle the situation presented, your head will be punched in and you could lose your life.

These last practices deal with Mastering the Space in your mind. They have been practiced for thousands of years, and you will find many variances according to different teachers of different traditions. Don't get too hung up on who taught what, or thinking you can't follow tradition A because you started with tradition B: they can all work if you practice any one of them diligently. But please try using only meditation technique at a time. When you do decide on one technique, follow it thoroughly for at least 3 months before giving it up. Lastly, while you are doing one technique in a single session, do not mix it up with another! That would be the equivalent of trying to straight arm bar and choke someone at the same time! Just make a commitment that you will do one technique for the entire sitting session.

SITTING MEDITATION

I would be willing to bet that if you took a study of successful people in the world, you would find there are certain daily traits they perform on a regular basis. I would put my money down that a daily constant practice of meditation is probably one of the most important and practiced traits from successful people. There have been thousands upon thousands of studies done on meditation. There is a reason why this practice has been around for so long. To put it bluntly, meditation when practiced with regularity, can positively impact your life.

MEDITATION TECHNIQUE 1 (ALSO KNOWN AS NOBODY CARES ABOUT YOUR CHAKRAS)

Designate a time of at least 8 but no more than 20 minutes to yourself. Make sure the area around you is clear of any distractions. It doesn't have to be an altar or anything like that, although it can be if you believe in that sort of thing. Ultimately though, this meditation technique is a mind practice, and for a mind practice to work, all you need is your mind. It's that simple.

First, relax. Does that direction sound incredibly simple? That's because it is and yet when you try to do it, you will discover it is not as easy as it seems. To put it in terms that youngsters might use, you need to just chill out. Let go of whatever idea you might have about what meditation should be like. If this is your first time doing meditation, please let go of any preconceived notions you may have about it. YOU MUST LET YOUR MIND BE AS IT IS.

Don't fall into the trap of thinking your meditation should be a certain way. There is an incredibly high chance that your actual meditation will be different than what you think. You might not feel euphoric, happy, or any sense of peacefulness at all. There is an extremely high chance that meditation will be excruciatingly boring. Get used to it. Be innocent and accept each moment as it comes without guilt, judgment, or fear.

The technique of basic mindfulness is incredibly simple. Sit comfortably on a cushion or the front part of a chair so your back is straight. Have your eyes either half closed, looking down, or fully closed. Focus your attention on the area of your nostrils. Feel the air coming in and out. It may be incredibly subtle and hard to notice at first. That's okay. Just relax and do your best. If you find yourself pushing or trying too hard, work on relaxing a little more.

If you find you are super relaxed and completely daydreaming, relax again, accept your mind as it is, and come back to the sensation of the breath at your nostrils. It may become very localized once you find the sensation of the air. You might find it on the upper lip, or the inner part of the nostril. Be kind to yourself and wherever you find it, just keep on observing what you feel.

It's like you don't care what comes up in the mind. You're going to do your best yet not be too concerned if your mind just so happens to wander from the sensation of the breath. Yes, you are going to experience thoughts sooner or later. That's fine. When you have thoughts and you notice them, just gently come back to the feeling of the air coming in and out of your nostrils. You might notice it for a fleeting second, but then it'll disappear and you'll be mired in your thoughts again. That's okay. Just keep coming back to the localized feeling of the breath coming in and out of your nose.

At this point, you might find yourself criticizing this technique. Why the hell should I do this? What does this guy know? If I'm not experiencing 100% pure bliss, then why should I even practice? Where are my chakras at? Why aren't they appearing?

Here's the truth about meditation: those who claim to have "no thoughts" or bliss all the time are either liars or really enlightened people. Frankly, I don't think even the most enlightened folk are perfect all the time either.

The point of all this (indeed, the benefit of all this practice) is **NOT** to enter completely thought free zones, although you might experience that from time to time. The goal is not to attain some permanent bliss, although you might experience momentary periods of that. The real benefit of meditation of any sort is the **redefining of your relationship with your thoughts**. That's basically it. There are several dozens, if not hundreds, of meditation techniques. The gist of most mindfulness style techniques is two-fold. One, you develop a certain type of "mindfulness" into whatever area you're focusing on. And yes, with mindfulness comes a certain type of concentration which can induce moments of calm and peace in the body and mind. But more importantly, **mindfulness meditation allows you to be friendlier with your mind.**

As you become friendlier with your own mind, you start to unravel and use the prefix of Jiu Jitsu in your life. "Jiu" in Jiu Jitsu refers to harmonization with external things, not fighting them. Applying meditation to your life is one of the best examples of Inner Jiu Jitsu. You're simply using the physical principles of outer Jiu Jitsu on your own mind. **You also must practice the same kind of diligence and patience with yourself that you accept with Outer Jiu Jitsu. Does it make sense to be so judgmental to yourself if you can't master a new technique in one practice session? Do you quit and say, "*This technique doesn't work, it sucks.*"** Most likely the answer is no. So don't apply this immaturity towards meditation.

We go through life consciously or unconsciously at odds with our thoughts, which in essence means we are at odds with our own mind. There is usually an undercurrent of antagonism of being at odds with our own self so to speak. We either want more of something if it is pleasurable or less of something that is undesirable.

We are enslaved by our thoughts, and it is why we seek "spiritual" improvement in the first place. Real spirituality is designed for you to truly be friends with yourself. You are still going to have all sorts of thoughts and feelings, some pleasant and not so pleasant. But as you start to recognize your thoughts and accept them as they are, the power of the thought process becomes less of a burden. You realize you don't have to let them influence you unless you choose to. This is *freedom* in the ultimate sense. It reminds me of the oft-quoted Art of

War by Sun Tzu: *Know your enemy*. **Most of the time, our enemy is our mind. So get to know your mind in all its craziness, quirkiness, and aversions. Know it so well that it no longer becomes your enemy but your best friend.**

IF you achieve this understanding, then congratulations! You really will be a Master of your Space! This freedom comes in tiny moments usually. But when it happens, it's the truest sense of freedom you can feel! For a moment, you can actually not be a slave to your thoughts and emotions. You can choose your destiny.

Jiu Jitsu allows you to choose an outcome you normally would not get otherwise. Without Jiu Jitsu, you get your ass kicked and are controlled by the person attacking you. With the skill of Jiu Jitsu, you can survive and even achieve a win! Using these principles of freeing your mind is the ultimate victory and an incredible use of your Inner Jiu Jitsu!

MEDITATION TECHNIQUE 2: METTA PRACTICE

This next practice comes from the Buddhist tradition, but as with many Buddhist practices, it is universal and secular in its application. The power of this practice is truly underestimated in its impact on our lives, the way we feel, and of course how we might potentially treat others. I offer this practice to you as a Gold Standard practice. Please do not take it lightly.

This practice can be done almost anywhere, including while you are driving. It is divided into 3 phases with only 4 lines. There are many versions of this practice, but I offer the version I was originally taught. Of course, you can modify and change as needed but the core will stay the same.

PHASE 1- METTA FOR ONESELF

What is Metta? Metta is a Pali word that is broad in scope but simple in meaning. It's the feeling or intention of wishing friendliness, well-being, love, non-harm, or any positive feeling onto a living being. Phase one of Metta practice begins at generating positive feelings towards oneself. It might seem silly, but many people misconstrue compassion as always thinking about others at the exclusion of oneself. This is simply incorrect and illogical. Love and kindness must start with oneself. The positive traits of self-appreciation, self-care, and self-love are very important.

Why is it important to start with yourself? I stated above that if Metta does not start with oneself, it is simply illogical. Why is that? Well, the gist of this book is that in order to perform at your very best, you must come from a state of mind that is not negative or weak. Here again, I will quote Gandhi, "You must *be* the change you seek in the world." If we really do want to help others, it makes sense to actually BE a great person to instill greatness in others.

The first phase of Metta towards oneself is a path towards becoming a better person. Otherwise, our practice of helping others will be weak or not as effective as it could be. In other words, it would be selfish in the truest sense of the word to *not* start with Metta practice for oneself because you're ultimately shortchanging your altruistic power. So do Metta for yourself for two reasons. First, it will make you feel amazing. Second, by feeling amazing, you will perform as a better human for the rest of the universe. I believe the Dalai Lama calls this idea "wise selfishness." It's a beautiful twist on the normal understanding of the word "selfish" because it shows an understanding of our interdependence with the rest of the world. Helping yourself first can ultimately help others with the right intention.

The Metta practice starts with four short phrases:

May I be happy
May I be free from suffering
May I be free from hatred
May I be able to protect my own happiness

There are longer versions that get more detailed and specific, but I like the brevity of this. Although you can do this anytime and pretty much anywhere, I personally like to do it in the morning after my mindfulness meditation. However, I've done this in my car, walking down the hallways, and at random times when I am not getting along with people and need a boost of positivity. It's simple. You just keep repeating it over and over again until you start to feel positive intention build up in your body and mind. When you contemplate the lines, you can use any visualization that you find appropriate. The visualizations should be natural and feel right to you. As long as you feel the energy of happiness, love, and kindness surround you and flow in and out of you, you can't go wrong.

Spending at least 4-8 minutes is a surefire way to feel the positive effects of this practice. Not only do you feel happier, but you also start to feel a protective shield, thanks to the 4th line, that lessens the impacts of anger and other negative impediments.

Sacred Summary For Phase 1 Metta

Remember, in the end, the better you feel and the happier you are, the better you will perform and act in life. At the very least, feeling happy has great value in and of itself. So whether you win or not in a match, you'll react with a different quality of experience in the long run.

PHASE 2- METTA FOR OTHERS

The second phase of Metta is directing and channeling all the positive energy to others. The lines are similar to the first with just a change of intent and direction to where the energy is flowing to. It goes like this:

May others be happy
May others be free from suffering
May others be free from enmity
May others be able to protect their own happiness

This second phase can be directed towards those you love at first. You can direct it toward your family and close friends. Starting with those you love helps generate the feelings outward. We don't want to jump into sending love and positive feelings towards strangers until we feel that we can honestly do so. It's easy to send kindness to those we love and are close to.

Again, you can visualize in any way that feels right to you. Sometimes, the word "visualize" frightens some people as they think they aren't imaginative enough to do this, or they simply aren't a visual type of person. If you think you aren't a person that can visualize or imagine well, then just try to get a feel for the loving-kindness to spread to your loved ones. Metta is a feeling anyways, so as long as you're feeling it, that's all that matters.

If you wish to proceed with the Metta to others, you can start to spread it to anyone you respect or care about. This can go for your teachers, family friends, or people you don't know too well but like anyway. Maybe it's the nice server at Starbucks who greets you with a smile, or the person at the grocery store that goes out of their way for you. Maybe it's the people at your Jiu Jitsu gym that practice with you but you don't know too much about.

The final part of spreading Metta to others at this stage is to send it out to people you feel neutral about. This, of course, can be the vast amounts of strangers that we meet but whose names we do not know. Metta is limited only by your sense of limitation. Since your imagination is limitless, you really have an unlimited amount of Metta to give.

Sacred Summary for Phase 2 Metta

Send loving kindness to the people you truly care and respect the most. Then go from the people you love to people who you like but don't know too much about. Finally, give out your positive feelings to those you have no feelings good or bad for, like the innumerable strangers we encounter in a single day.

PHASE 3- METTA FOR ENEMIES (OTHERWISE KNOWN AS BECOMING A GOD)

This is by far, the hardest part of Metta. I would say don't try this until you feel authentic in your practice. That's why it's important to start easy with the ones you love and your friends. You work past those you like to neutral people, then finally to people you dislike or despise.

The cool thing is that as you start to really engage Metta for yourself (phase 1), you gain a confidence and power you never dreamed of. Visualizing and empowering your practice with self-care gives you a healing sense of invincibility. It's not based on an invincibility from outward enemies in a physical sense, but rather from a sense of total self-worth that obliterates any self-induced fears. If you generate enough Self Metta, you will find your sense of self so expansive that it encompasses all beings in the universe including your own enemies. This does make you feel invincible because your enemies no longer can affect you in any negative manner. You are free from their influence. That is real power.

To work Metta for your enemies, you simply imagine the person who caused you stress or pain and use a correct pronoun:

May he/she be happy
May he/she be free from suffering
May he/she be free from enmity
May he/she be able to protect her own happiness

Again, use any visualization that works. One effective way to do this is by imagining beams of light emanating from your heart center and spreading into the person's body and soul. Visualization is part imagination and also part feeling. Combining those two traits is ideal and one usually leads to the other.

It's obvious that this is a courageous and possibly difficult practice because our enemies can really be a nuisance in our lives. People may have done some horribly destructive things to us or people we love. I certainly struggle with this practice a ton. There is one practice however that can help you overcome the hurdle of feeling like you can't do it: **BECOME A GOD**.

To become a god comes from the Tantric tradition and is known as Deity Yoga. To do this, you have to meet a guru from an authentic tradition, get initiated, and make a pledge to do the practice. The practice includes intense and detailed visualizations, sacred mantras, and mudras. The most important thing though is the taking on of a belief that YOU ARE NOT A LIMITED HUMAN BEING, BUT RATHER A SUPERNATURAL BEING OF LIGHT. You really take on the belief that your TRUE NATURE is one of divinity and power and that the human flesh body is the illusionary body. Once you take on the belief AS IF you are truly a god/goddess/deity, you operate from that as your normal base. Think of the limitless power to help others with this as your normal operating system! If you really were a deity, with a thousand arms and cosmic powers to take on the pains and sufferings of the world, would you be afraid? Why would you be afraid? There would be nothing to be afraid of. With your unlimited power, you would work tirelessly to help those in need because you would not be you, **you** would be a luminous being.

The idea of deity yoga is timeless and universal in all systems of self-improvement. Yes, there is the formal procedure of meeting a guru and following all the rules of the tradition from ancient India. However, the basic secular formula that we all can do without a guru is this: **TAKE ON THE ATTITUDE THAT YOU ARE BIGGER THAN WHAT YOU SEEM.** You have to take on the attitude that if you operate from a larger sense of self as your **true nature**, then the sky is the limit in what you can achieve. It's important to not let this idea bloat your ego because the results could be disastrous to yourself and others. For goodness sakes, don't become a Jim Jones type nut job. However, with self-awareness and balanced confidence, you should periodically take on the idea that you are something incredible, a force for good, with infinite love and an intention to help others. It's just living the words of Master Yoda: "*Luminous beings we are, not this crude matter.*" I remember while studying at the monastery in Woodstock, New York, Khenpo Karthar Rinpoche said the exact same thing in Tibetan. My heart exploded with joy when I heard him say that. Use this idea of deity yoga in competition as well.

LAST PHASE- METTA FOR ALL LIFE EVERYWHERE

Finally, the last step of Metta is to spread all your happiness, all your safety, all your protection to all beings in the universe. At this stage, you release all limitations on the amount of happiness you have and unleash your love to every single being in the universe! There are no rules in how far you can go in your positive intent and sharing of positive life-enhancing energy. Have a little bit of fun with it and simply let it go!

May all beings be happy
May all beings be free from suffering
May all beings be free from hatred
May all beings be able to protect their own happiness

Now I kept the Metta practice very simple with just four lines to be repeated. However, you really can go as deep and particular as you want. Perhaps it is better health you want for another person. In that case, then just add, "May I be healthy." Maybe it's safety you wish to bestow. Just change the words to say, "May he/she be safe." You can be specific to mental health and say, "May I be mentally healthy and free from distress."

Is the word, "enmity" too strong for you? Then just change it to "resentment" instead. Some of us really do carry a feeling of enmity or hatred around with us, but for many, we're just annoyed or resentful. It's a lesser form of hatred. Finally, you can also just be very general and say, "May I live in this world happy, joyfully, and at ease."

In conclusion, Metta practice is one of the most healing practices we can perform for ourselves. It makes you feel loved, cared for, confident, self-assured, and wonderful overall. It makes you feel strong and expands your sense of self when you spread it to others. The reason why I include this as a technique is because not only will your athletic performance be enhanced, but you'll be a better human being in general.

When I do Metta before Jiu Jitsu practice, I actually roll better. It's because I'm rolling from a better state of mind. My techniques get better because I'm more relaxed. I also listen to my teachers' instructions better. If you haven't realized it yet, what affects the mind will affect the body. So these mental techniques will make you a better competitor, more successful, more peaceful, less stressed, and an overall greater human being. I think these attributes can easily carry over into the workplace as well as our personal lives. What's more spiritual than that?

Once again, I offer these practices because they are great examples of the efficiency of energy, and they serve as a reflection of the principles of Jiu Jitsu overall. Jiu Jitsu (and all martial arts in general) should serve to make us better human beings. If they don't, we are simply not using our skills to their highest level. It's like only getting to brown belt and stopping there. To become a master of martial arts, you have to go beyond the physical aspects and journey deep into the Inner dimension. When you do, your understanding of outer Jiu Jitsu becomes stronger and much more profound.

SUMMARY FOR METTA PRACTICE: When you perform Metta for yourself and others, you'll feel better in general. The better YOU feel, the greater you'll perform and act towards others in the long run!

CHAPTER

4

KNOWING YOUR CENTER IS KNOWING YOUR LIFE AND CONTROLLING YOUR CENTER IS CONTROLLING YOUR LIFE

O FTENTIMES IN JIU Jitsu, we find ourselves in a situation like the one in the following photos. In this case, if you are on the bottom and can manipulate the opponent's arms so that they cross the imaginary centerline of the body, then you will dominate. In contrast, if you are the one who gets his arm crossed past center, then you will be controlled. Our goal is to always control the center of the opponent and never let our own center be compromised.

Figure 11: Here we see Judo Olympian Charlee Minkin on top holding her center perfectly just like she should when defending the guard.

Figure 12: But now a terrible thing has happened, Charlee has let her arm cross her centerline. Once the centerline is compromised, you can be manipulated.

Figure 13: In this case, the mighty Charlee is literally swept. Similarly, you might get "swept" in life if you let your core values get compromised.

Figure 14: Jiu Jitsu World League Champion Ben Lowry is now in the dominant position. If you control your center, you control your life!

This is the easiest to promote in terms of metaphors then. Controlling your center is a call to know yourself, your values, and your place in the world. When you operate from this sense of controlling the center, you will operate from your highest sense of self. You will naturally attract more things that are in touch with that sense of self. Don't be surprised if after doing these sets of exercises, you find yourself with a new job, a new business partner, or a new love.

FIRST BUILD A SENSE OF CENTER

Let's go on a journey of discovering our values which will build a pillar of what our center is all about. Once you do this, you'll create a new center of gravity. From that new sense of you, your entire universe will change and you'll attract things that are more attuned to your values. Your very existence will change and create a new chain of consequences that will be more life-enhancing than you could dream of.

If you haven't done an exercise like this before, there's a very good chance you're living with an invisible sense of values that haven't been articulated or brought to light yet. However, the danger is that you're not aware of what's driving you in the ultimate sense. Or you might know what you want in life, but you won't understand *why you want it*. It could very easily be manipulated by circumstances outside yourself in which case you'll be like the person swept or choked by letting their arm getting crossed over.

Ask yourself these questions to distinguish two sets of values. The first will be called **OPTIMIZING VALUES** and the other will be called **NEGATIVE VALUES**.

1. What feelings have been most important to you in life?

Think of all the feelings you have valued in the past? If you find yourself valuing *things*, then think about what is the feeling associated with the thing that you value? For example, if you value a fast car, perhaps the feeling you associate with that car is *joy*. If you value money, perhaps the feeling you associate with it is *safety* or *confidence*.

To help you draw out more distinction between these types of values ask yourself the second question:

2. In the past, what has been more important for you to feel? _____ or _____?

As you answer the second question, start thinking about the hierarchy of which values matter more than others. Rank them. Create a list of at least 7 core optimizing values that you really care about.

Finally, ask yourself this question:

3. In the past, what had to happen in order for you to feel _____?

These positive values are ultimately going to optimize your life. They will bring greater satisfaction and joy. They will augment the positive factors in your life and attract more of the same qualities.

Now think about the factors that take you away from your values. What are the emotional states you would like to avoid? These are what I call **negative values**. It's self-explanatory. They are negative because they ultimately take you away from your values. They keep you off center and make you weak and vulnerable.

Ask yourself these questions to draw out your negative values:

1. In the past, what have been the feelings you would do everything you could to avoid having to feel? (Create a list.)

Again, here is the simple question to help you distinguish a ranking system of your negative values:

2. In the past, which of these feelings would you avoid feeling the most? _____ or
_____?

Make a list of your negative values and rank them. Put a 1 next to your absolute worst value and rank the rest accordingly.

3. The final question is to continue to draw nuance to your value system: What has to happen in order for you feel _____
_____?

You'll notice that all of these questions were prefixed by "in the past." In order to be your best self and operate from your ultimate core, you need to create an extremely compelling sense of purpose and destiny. What do you truly want to be? What do you ultimately want to succeed at in life?

HAVING A STRONG CENTER MEANS HAVING A COMPELLING VISION MAP FOR YOUR FUTURE!

1. Imagine for a moment what it would be like to have anything you would like in life? Brainstorm through as many items as you can about what you would like to do, have, achieve, create, give, or experience in the next 20 years. DO NOT HOLD BACK!! Do you hold back in Jiu Jitsu when someone's

trying to sweep you by breaking your center? HELL NO! So maintain and create a stronger center by unleashing your wish list to the universe! Write all of your wishes down in a notebook.

2. Determine how much time you think it will take to accomplish each goal. Go back through your list and write 1, 3, 5, 10, or 20 years next to each item.

3. Be scrupulous and reassess your list again. Choose your top 3 or 4 one year goals. Clarify with detail why you absolutely will achieve these goals. Take as much space in your notebook as you need.

4. FINALLY, write down what kind of person would you need to become to achieve all the wonderful things you wanted from number one on this list. Describe in great detail the **values, actions, character traits, qualities, beliefs, virtues, habits**, etc., this incredible being would have to embody to accomplish all that you wrote.

CREATE YOUR NEW OPTIMIZED VALUE LIST

As you look back on your old values, how do you feel about them? Do you feel good with the way they are ranked in your life? Do they make you feel empowered? Are there some that you feel could be changed either in order or could some be thrown out with new ones? Do the following to start the process towards a new value list that can change your future!

1. CLARIFY YOUR DESTINY. This again relates to the last point on our previous list. What kind of person or character

do you actually want to become in this lifetime? What do you want your life to really be about?

2. CLARIFY YOUR VALUES. What order do your highest values need to be in to achieve your ultimate destiny?

3. View your current list and question yourself: What do you gain by having your values in this order?

4. COST- Could this particular order cost you by distracting you away from your destiny?

5. Do you need to eliminate any values in order to achieve your ultimate destiny?

6. Are there other values you need to add in order to achieve your ultimate destiny?

7. If you create new values, what order do those values need to be in order to build your destiny/center?

8. Be CERTAIN that there is no conflict in the hierarchy of your values.

DESIGN YOUR NEW NEGATIVE VALUE LIST

Knowing what your positive optimizing values consist of brings you clarity on what you really want as your destiny, but knowing the things that can take it away are equally important. You want to have a good understanding of the feelings and emotional states that will take you off your center and away from your destiny. This way, you can preemptively protect yourself whenever these states come your way and avoid consistent dwelling in these adverse emotional areas.

Brainstorm a list of **negative** values based on the following question:

What emotional states do you need to avoid spending too much time in so you can achieve your ultimate lifestyle?

Which negative values do you need to avoid the most in order to achieve your ultimate life plan? (In other words, put your negative values in a hierarchal list.)

If you put your heart and soul into this, CONGRATULATIONS! You've made yourself a new sense of center that will hold you when anyone or anything tries to "sweep" or "submit" you in life!

THE POWER OF RELATIONSHIPS

Now that you have a basic idea of your value system, let's see an application of it in a real situation. Let's try it in relationships.

Relationships, in my opinion, are the single most important factor in life. You can have all the money in the world, but if you are alone, it sucks. You can be the poorest person in the world, but if you have someone that loves you and cares about you, it makes the world a little more bearable. Think about the times when you've had most of your day going great but you got in a really bad argument with your lover. How does that affect you? Are you able to stay on top of the world when your relationship is hurting? The answer is no. There is no reason why we shouldn't make relationships an important factor in life. As with all things, it stands to reason that if you are in a great relationship, you might just perform better in all other endeavors, including Jiu Jitsu.

This exercise can be done whether you're currently in a relationship and want to upgrade it or it can be used preemptively to find a very compatible soul mate.

Just like you did for your ultimate life destiny above, have a notebook ready!

1. First, define the ideal perfect mate. Unleash in great detail all the things you would love to have in an intimate relationship. What would they be like? What would they talk about? What would they look like? How would their personality be? What kind of career would they have? What would their values be like? What would their mental, spiritual, and physical traits be like for you? Hold nothing back! Pretend it's Christmas Eve and you get to wish for whatever you want.

2. Now look at your detailed list and start to single out the *absolute* musts. Star or highlight some of the things that you *absolutely must have* in a relationship. Obviously, it would be hard to find someone who fits every single criterion you create but with this list, you will be able to narrow it down to things that mean the most to you.

3. To create some more energy and refinement in this, create a list of values you absolutely CANNOT STAND in a relationship. What would the most hellish version of a mate be for you? Write it down! What character, actions, values, or personality traits do you absolutely despise so much that it would feel like a violation of your being to be in a relationship with this person?

4. The last step is the most empowering. Ask yourself, what do **YOU HAVE TO BECOME IN ORDER TO ATTRACT YOUR SUPER MATE?** What kind of personality do you have to have to attract this kind of mate? What values would you

have to uphold? What kind of body would you have to have to attract the physical qualities you desire? Ultimately, it comes back to becoming the thing you wish to attract! **Be the change you seek in the world!**

When you finish this, you'll probably have the same reaction I had when I did it the first time. First, it's fun. Second, it's simple. Third, as simple as it is, it brings about incredible clarity and vision about what you really like in a relationship. Can you imagine the state of the world if they taught this simple process in high school? Is there any surprise why this country has such a high divorce rate? What ends up happening for most of us is that we get caught up in the initial passion and excitement of a relationship without ever knowing who the person is we're entangled with. If we don't take the time to delineate our core values, we will find ourselves easily swept up in the cognitive dissonance of mundane relationships.[6]

---

6   My meditation instructor's partner has many books on this subject. She is a master of relationships. Check out her work http://barbaradeangelis. com/

LEVERAGE AND SEIRYOKU ZENYO[7]

THE CONCEPT OF leverage is extremely simple. Yet, like so many things, it is extremely profound and deep.

The entire focus of Brazilian Jiu Jitsu is based on leverage.

---

7   Here is Kano Sensei's definition-"Seiryoku-Zenyo (maximum efficient use of energy) applies to all types of endeavours, and it is to fully utilize one's spiritual and physical energies to realise an intended purpose.

Seiryoku-Zenyo is the most effective use of the power of the mind and body. In the case of Judo, this is the principle upon which attack and defense are based, and what guides the process of teaching as well. Simply, the most effective use of mind and body may be described as the maximum efficient utilization of energy. In summary, this can be described as 'maximum efficiency'.

This idea of the best use of energy is one of the central tenets in Judo, **but it is also important for achieving various aims in one's life**." 1 Kano Jigoro, "The Best Use of Energy", Taisei, Vol.1, No.1, 1922.

If you find the right leverage points on a sweep, submission, or takedown, you take control of the situation regardless of the size of the opponent. Leverage is what Rickson Gracie (for those who don't know Rickson, he's the Michael Jordan of Jiu Jitsu) stated in an interview once as being the pinnacle of Jiu Jitsu. It's what allows a weaker, smaller, individual to defeat a bigger, stronger adversary. This becomes the ultimate metaphor for life.

The concept of leverage starts with the idea of using a tool, namely a *lever*, to manipulate another object, in a way that benefits the user and in a way that overcomes otherwise impossible circumstances. Take the use of a crowbar for example. It's a device that allows for opening doors of even the sturdiest of material. Outside of this simple example though, leverage is the skill to maximize influence on a person, situation, or event to our advantage.

In Jiu Jitsu, we turn our elbows, feet, hips, knees, and even our head into that crowbar. All forms of Jiu Jitsu, Judo, and even Aikido and Tai Chi are initially based on the laws of the physical world. These laws can be manipulated with a little sense and know how.

Look at the most basic mount escape, so simple that it is taught in the first class of any Jiu Jitsu school:

Figure 15: These photos demonstrate the power of leverage in life. When you maximize your energy in the most efficient ways possible, you can start to shape the life you want on your terms. Even the great and larger Master Rigan Machado can get rolled!

Figure 16: Now instead of being on the "bottom" of life, Professor Nobu has demonstrated the skillful technique of maximum efficiency to achieve a life on your own terms. You create the life you want out of your own intention when you channel your mind and body to maximum optimization of life's situations.

If we disregard the physical aspect of the concept, then leverage becomes a term that can encompass more than we dreamed of. We can use *anything, in a way that maximizes the greatest benefit to the user to achieve otherwise unattainable ends*. When one masters leverage, one is simply unstoppable. Leverage is the closest thing to having a super power. It is the Secret behind all Secrets. Lucky for us though, it's not magic in the sense of it being unnatural. In fact, it's quite the opposite. Leverage is the most natural functioning law there is. You just have to discover it.

The big question is:

WHAT ARE YOUR LEVERAGE POINTS IN LIFE?

If Jiu Jitsu is about using and creating levers, than this whole book is about the same skill on a daily basis when life is challenging you. Obviously, the text should be used a lot when you are a beginner. As time goes on, you will find that you can discover levers in your life on your own.

If you have not read or studied the works of Master Jigoro Kano, the founder of Judo, I highly recommend that you do. Kano Sensei was one of the greatest martial artists of all time. He had the ability to organize and systematize the physical with the spiritual. His emphasis on maximum efficiency to better oneself or achieve one's goal was simply astounding.

This idea is inspiring to all who wish to be successful. It is not just constantly "yielding" (*ju yoku go o seisu*) to one's opponent when he or she is being aggressive. This is a stereotype based off the word "jiu" in Jiu Jitsu. Yes, there is a time and place for that but Master Kano argues that this isn't the universal idea of the "Jiu" in Jiu Jitsu. Rather, the true universal message behind his work that could be applied at all times is *seiryoku zenyo* (Using one's mind and body in the most efficient and effective way possible).

Read with open ears and an empty mind these words from the master:

"One's mental and physical energy must be used most effectively in order to achieve a certain goal. That is to say, one must apply the most effective method or technique for using the mind and body. If we use the term 'seiryoku' for one's mental and physical energy, this should be expressed as seiryoku saizen katsuyo (best use of one's energy). We can shorten this to seiryoku zenyo (maximum efficiency). This means that no matter what the goal, in order to achieve it, you must put your mental and physical energy to work in the most effective manner." (Kano, 2005, pg. 43)

Understanding this is truly the golden ticket. This is making "magic" real in your life. It is the great unifying force of secular thought and so called mystical thinking. If you take this as your guiding star, it can be applied to everything in life.

The Inner Jiu Jitsu concepts of Seiryoku Zenyo and leverage are all about using the inherent natural flow of energy in oneself, one's opponent, and one's environment to what is most advantageous to the situation and to the practitioner. It sounds very general, and it starts off that way, but the key is to find as many ways to apply it as possible.

When I studied at Naropa University, we were predominantly influenced by Tibetan Buddhists. Their tradition has a philosophy that can be quite complicated and difficult to understand, but it also has displays of simple wisdom. If you ever want to explore Tibetan Buddhism, then you need to get your hands on a translation of The Root Text of the Seven Points of Training the Mind. There are many different versions out there. Pema Chodron has some really wonderful commentary on it and so does her teacher Chogyam Trungpa Rinpoche. This text is really about becoming friends with yourself and all those around you. When you do that, you alleviate a lot of heavy baggage that you might not even know you are carrying. Not only that, but you break limitations of what you feel you can accomplish because you lessen your fears.

The reason I bring this up is because it is my belief that spirituality should be something that builds you up in life. Not only that, but it should be pleasurable to some extent. Yes, there are arduous training periods where you experience very little in the way of gains (especially when compared to the amount of suffering and sacrifice you go through), but ultimately, it's something that should feel good and natural. There are many purists who would definitely dispute me on this position, but I stand by my claim.

It's the same in Jiu Jitsu. We do Jiu Jitsu for many reasons, but one of the most important reasons is because it's fun. In fact, it's one of the most fun things to do with your time. Spirituality should have a little bit of fun to it as well. After all, it is a way for you to feel more alive. If you have that mindset for both activities, your involvement in them will stay strong.

Many would say the spiritual life is about crushing the ego and therefore bringing you down. Again, there is a time and place for that, but this book is written from the point of view of a householder. What I mean by that is we have to *build up our ego* to a healthy functioning position, not destroy it. I feel outer Jiu Jitsu does this by making us feel more secure with ourselves in a self-defense situation.

Using leverage in life then is using every available tool at your disposal to accomplish your goals. Spirituality is a lever if it lightens your personality and makes you a happier person.

Having your finances in order makes you less stressed (and, therefore, happier) because you can focus your money on things you want to do instead of being dominated by feelings of lack.

Having good time management is a great way to demonstrate efficiency. People who prepare the day before and who leave earlier to get to work, are masters of applying Seiryoku Zenyo and leverage to their lives. Business leaders who are constantly anticipating changes in technology are great at practicing Seiryoku Zenyo and leverage.

Being in good relationships with your family, friends, and loved ones are great examples of Seiryoku Zenyo and leverage. It goes without saying that handling one's obstacles in the most efficient manner is also good Seiryoku Zenyo and leverage.

Now that you have an idea of what constitutes Maximum Efficiency and Leverage, you should understand the opposite of what NOT applying efficiency and leverage to your life could be.

For example, I complain like the best of them, and occasionally it makes me feel better. But if I were to look at myself honestly, I would realize it's a giant waste of time and energy. If I don't have the ability to change the situation, what good will it do to complain?

The same thing goes for talking too much and arguing. Again, there is a time and place for arguing. But what about arguing out of anger? Sure, I suppose we can rationalize anger at certain times, but do we use it in that way often? Usually, these types of behavior result in a waste of energy and do not demonstrate good Seiryoku Zenyo or leverage.

Finally, look at how we use our time on Facebook, Social Media, or the internet. The time spent on these things can often be dreadful, petty, gossipy, and definitely not helpful to us in any major way.

Mundane Ways that Express the efficiency of Seiryoku Zenyo in Everyday Life vs. Not being in the spirit of Seiryoku Zenyo

Cooking breakfast while coffee brews	Mindlessly scrolling on Facebook (probably the number one antithesis of efficiency)
Having your clothes wash or dry while you clean your house, or preparing your clothes the night before	Letting household chores build up so that you are forced to do a bunch which impedes on your freedom and makes you feel overloaded with dread
Performing Standing Meditation while waiting in line	Getting frustrated and anxious over a situation you have no control over
Learning from a podcast in the car while you drive	Mindlessly scrolling station past station of the radio in hopes that something good sounding will come your way
Forgiving your parents (assuming it frees up psychological trauma so you can perform better in life)	Holding onto grudges and resentment over people to the point where it consistently impinges on your life choices and reactions
Being positive and grateful in most situations	Complaining and blaming is a surefire way to lose your sense of power

Being kind	Being negative and mean simply drops everyone into a lower performing state
Living a life of deliberate design with clear and specific goals	Living from a state or feeling dominated by forces beyond your control. A life of constant reaction by a sense that things are being done to you, not for you, with no sense of self-autonomy or control.

The last example is the one we are going to attempt the most as it is the overall goal of Inner Jiu Jitsu!

EXERCISE TO DETERMINE YOUR LEVERAGE

Let's do a simple exercise to see where you are in terms of having good leverage in your life and what you could do to improve it.

Think back to the moment you woke up today until now. For the next five minutes (set a timer), write down as many things as you can remember that were positive in nature, made you feel better, used your time wisely, or helped you in a particular positive goal or state of being. Be brief. If you can't decide whether something was positive or not, it probably wasn't. If it feels good writing it, and you felt happy when you did it, then it probably deserves to be on the list. Trust your instincts with this.

Stop reading now and do the exercise for five minutes.

So glad that you are back! Now let's do another list. This time, think back on your day and write down the moments that did not serve you. These are things that wasted your time, made you feel upset, did not create a positive feeling, or left you feeling less freedom.

Go take another five minutes and write it down.

Now before we beat ourselves up over our list because of our presumptive attitude of what it should be instead of what it is, let's just take a moment and analyze it objectively. We will never be perfect; **we just need to be spectacular in our effort to try.**

How do you feel about your list? What parts would you change to better optimize your life so you can feel more secure? Do you wish you spent less time on certain behaviors and more with others? What actions did you list that wasted your time and energy? Were there some actions that started positively but then slipped into something that brought you down?

As you contemplate this, you are planting the seeds for better efficiency in your life. Once again, awareness starts the journey.

APPLYING LEVERAGE IN LIFE EXERCISE

In Jiu Jitsu, it is a good idea to avoid exposing the back because it can lead to someone punching, choking you from behind. Life can really suck here. It can often lead to defeat from the person who has their back taken. However, there is still a way to improve your position. With intelligence and strategy, you can get out. You still apply the philosophy of leverage.

How do you get the leverage you need in life? You make your chart, you list your pros and cons of your situation, but you don't end there. To really get the leverage you need, you need to use the pain and suffering of the situation to fuel you. IT IS ABSOLUTELY IMPERATIVE TO NOT BE PASSIVE AT THIS POINT. YOU MUST CHANGE YOUR PSYCHOLOGY. IN ORDER TO CHANGE YOUR PSYCHOLOGY, YOU MUST BE WILLING TO FEEL "PAIN".

To do this, you must be willing to imagine and feel what it would be like to be the thing you DO NOT WANT TO BE. If you're feeling uncomfortable just thinking about that, that's good.

Now imagine this: What do you NOT want in life? Imagine this in vivid detail. If you want a new relationship because you feel your current partner is absolutely nuts, IMAGINE and feel what it would be like to be with this person FOR THE REST OF YOUR LIFE. Do you want to get a new job because your current job leaves you passionless and feeling despondent? IMAGINE DYING WITH THIS JOB AS YOUR LAST OCCUPATION. Imagine the pain of lying on your deathbed, talking to your kids, trying to explain why you didn't accomplish your dreams or desires.

Think how your current excuses will seem so pathetic when you're trying to rationalize your failure to them. Imagine the pain you will feel knowing that you didn't live up to your potential. Set a timer and really feel the terror and pain of not accomplishing your dream for at least 5 minutes. WRITE DOWN ALL THE OUTCOMES OF THIS LIFE AND WHAT IT FEELS LIKE.

If this last part here is not making you feel uncomfortable, you have to visualize harder. You really have to hold nothing back and feel the true suffering. Pain drives people. To put it bluntly, pain can really suck. The good news is that because it sucks so badly, you will do whatever you can to get rid of it.

Now, assuming you've done the exercise properly, you should be in a pool of tears or vomit or both. However, you can now rejoice in some good news: we are not going to stay in this painful state. Pull yourself out and start writing about the pleasure of attaining your goals. Reverse the procedure and apply all the feelings of positive growth you will feel from doing the thing that you fear the most.

Go deep, visualize and feel the rewarding sense of accomplishment from getting your dreams! Make the image or feeling **brighter** and **bigger** in your mind! I must emphasize the idea of brightness in your visualization. Imagine your state as getting physically brighter. It will enhance your vision greatly.

Write down all the positive feelings you can associate with this transformed state. Then set the timer again and just imagine in your mind what it will feel like. Scream it out! Feel the joy! Don't hold back! Let it loose!

Another set of techniques that can bring about the power of leverage using pain is to communicate with others your intentions and make a promise in the form of a bet with them. Obviously, it has to be someone you really trust. Make the consequence of not accomplishing your goal extremely painful, immediate, but short-term. Some easy samples to work with are:

- Sending a shaming photo with commentary on social media about how you didn't accomplish your goal.

- Make the promise that if you don't carry out to your end result, you will send a check of at least 100 dollars to an organization you despise. It can be the political party you really hate for example. www.stickk.com is very effective and easy to use for this.

- Force yourself to do your least favorite exercise immediately to the point of exhaustion.

Whenever you finish your goal though, always have at least a mini-celebration of your accomplishment. Remember, pain has to used along with pleasure to get the best effects.

These exercises need to be done time and time again so you don't lose your momentum for growth. This is leverage. This is applying your natural responses to best change your life. When done with intelligence, you will escape your current negative circumstance and get to a new position of positive growth and potential. Do these exercises once a day, once a week, or at the very least once a month to keep yourself pushing upward in your personal development.

In outer Jiu Jitsu, we want to be a master of reactivity. We want to be able to know when to push and when to pull. There is a time to be aggressive, and a time to wait and react off the opponent. In the end, we do not want our opponent to control us. Similarly, in our Inner Jiu Jitsu, we seek to control our reactivity in ways that are most beneficial to us. Pain and pleasure are emotions that we can use with intelligence to accomplish our goals.

SUMMARY OF LEVERAGE AND SEIRYOKU ZENYO: Utilize as many circumstances in life to create optimal conditions that maximize your life, not diminish it. Whatever emotional obstacles hold you down, use them in a way that helps your life. Pain is a great teacher!

CHAPTER

6

CHANGING THE ANGLE-CHANGING THE MINDSET

THE ART OF Changing the Angle is profound. In many outer Jiu Jitsu cases, it seems initially that you are going into danger. In a sense you are. However, it's not done in a haphazard or bullheaded way. With the right amount of timing and intelligence, you change the angle, and suddenly the laws of physics work in your favor. Can there be a more apt metaphor of this for life?

In life, we are constantly beset by challenges. One of the greatest teachings I got on this came from the famous Buddhist teacher Pema Chodron and her teacher Chogyam Trungpa. They both had very deliberate titles behind a lot of their talks that hinted at the idea that turning INTO the so-called problem is the best path. The famous book, The Wisdom of No Escape, seems to nail this concept.

Both of these teachers (and many other wise people) have expounded this idea. In fact, one could argue that the entire spiritual teaching of the Mahayana vehicle of Buddhism is not one of retreating from life, but becoming more engaged with it. It also comes up in Tantric schools.[8]

At first glance, you might think this sounds crazy. Why on Earth would you move TOWARD pain and suffering instead of away from it? Why wouldn't you run away from it instead of engaging it? The answer is so simple if you understand the physical principles of outer Jiu Jitsu. If you have taken even a beginners course and done the aforementioned move of regaining guard from side mount, the answer will be obvious. With both emotional and spiritual intelligence, a trained practitioner can easily overcome the apparent obstacles in life with ease after some mental readjustment, perception change, and training.

All Jiu Jitsu practitioners can relate to the pressure of being crushed on the bottom from either a heavier opponent or a more skilled AND heavy opponent. This can be simply claustrophobic. But what does every good instructor say? 1. Relax 2. Believe you can get out 3. Use proper technique and you can get out.

The idea exists in the stand up striking arts as well. In all these arts, *it's only a matter of inches.*

This metaphor of changing the angle is all about the small but monumental positive changes a "few inches" can do. For example, if you decide tonight to wake up 20 minutes earlier for a consistent

---

8   There are Buddhist, Hindu, and even Jain versions of Tantra. Most forms are about embracing states of mind that are repulsive or rejected by mainstream society or religion. This includes negative emotions like anger and desire and transmuting them. It is a radical life affirming philosophy.

meditation practice, you will bring about a completely life changing consequence that will affect you forever. If you make a promise to spend 5 minutes a day identifying things you can be grateful for, you might enact a chain reaction of positive growth that can alter your life. If you make a strategic plan to save just $100 a month and invest it into a stock or account with a high compound interest rate, you might irrevocably produce an effect that could buy you financial freedom.

Your initial training in Jiu Jitsu might have started in this way. Perhaps you started the art of Jiu Jitsu as a small part time hobby. You didn't think it was going to have this huge impact on your life, but now look at yourself! You stay up late watching YouTube videos, going to tournaments, and staying up to date on the latest health trends to keep yourself in tip top shape.

The point is that most giant change starts with a small change that has a huge effect. Never underestimate small changes! They lead to giant growth over time!

Lastly, changing the angle is all about changing your attitude to the things that normally bring up fear and pain. When someone huge crushes their body on us in bottom side mount, our bodies initially feel the claustrophobia and pain. As we train, however, the small micro muscles in between our ribs get stronger and we can handle the pressure. We start to learn small movements like getting to our side that can greatly diminish the pain and pressure from the opponent on top. This obviously can be related to life.

Try experimenting with some of these scenarios in which you can confront situations that bring up discomfort. Change your mental angle on the situation and see if you can enact some positive long term benefits. Here are some examples:

- Next time you're at the doctor's office, ask if you can take a magazine from one of their waiting tables. It might make you feel uncomfortable at first, but then use that as a catalyst to test your mind's ability to "change the angle" for your overall benefit. It's not like you're stealing or hurting someone, so just try it!

- If you're arguing with your spouse or friend and feeling a sense of righteousness coming out of you that you're absolutely right, try and see the situation from the other's point of view (this is extremely hard to do)

- Think of something that makes you feel like you're a victim. Perhaps you suffered greatly from someone's financial decision, or you were physically harmed. Now try the seemingly impossible. Change the Angle of your thinking! Take on the possibility that Maybe, just maybe, life is working for you and not against you!

This last point has a huge amount of thought. Recently, I read an article about the reaction of two adopted children. The first child lived a life from the point of view that she was unloved, unlucky, and unworthy. The other child lived from the viewpoint that her life was a miracle. She felt she was handpicked by parents that loved her, that she had a purpose in her life, and that each moment had the potential to carry her further into knowing her purpose.

You've probably heard of similar such stories. The simple change in the self-made narrative, however, has giant consequences. These small changes of only a "few inches" can literally mean the difference between life and death for the martial artist, or a difference between a fully lived life and a life barely lived!

Figure 17: Notice the small amount of space readjustment that takes place here as the author barely moves his face from the path of the punch. This can reflect the small but much needed mental re-adjustment we must undertake to succeed in life.

Figure 18: This picture demonstrates the need to not run away from our problems but face into the pain. Of course, it must be done with skill and conscious intention. In this case, the author turns INTO the opponent with the left shoulder, stays balanced, yet is ready to counter strike in the situation of life. Professor Matt Cram on the right represents the obstacles and pains of life. The turning of the torso of the author on the left represents the skillful courage to face the problems, but with a new and better angle to succeed in the situation.

SUMMARY OF CHANGING THE ANGLE: Just like in outer Jiu Jitsu, small micro movements matter a lot! If you make small consistent changes in your life, you will reap giant rewards in the long run!

CHAPTER

7

THE BUDDHA HAD A SERIOUS INNER JIU JITSU GAME

BUDDHISM AND MARTIAL arts have often been equated or at least talked about as being connected. It's a huge stereotype seen in movies, television shows, books, and websites. (How many people have seen the story of how Jiu Jitsu was practiced by Buddhist monks before being transplanted to Brazil? It's not completely factual, but I digress). In any case, it's not a bad connection or an accidental one as many things in Buddhist literature can be a great lens to see Inner Jiu Jitsu and vice versa.

The key to change and success is to *Change our Angle of looking at the problem*! This Change of Angle or *change of perception* can be slight and subtle, or massive and overt. You have to apply your intelligence to your own situation. In essence, though, you have to question your narrative of reality. It may be a good narrative, but it ultimately does not equate to the only one there is. In fact, if you are even slightly biased, which of course we all are to some extent, your version of reality is going to be skewed as well.

This questioning of your perception is a decisive factor on relieving some stress off your psyche. It is what the seminal *Prajnaparamita Sutras* (ultimate wisdom texts) are about in Mahayana Buddhism. They consist of several thousand pages, but the only section that concerns us here is the Heart Sutra. According to the mythological conversations that accompany that text, there were many Buddhist monks that heard that sutra and experienced heart attacks.

The Heart Sutra is a strange but beautiful text on the possibility of changing your mental perceptions in life. Nothing is truly set in stone the way you think it is. There is always more room, more emptiness, and more potential for it to be something else.

Think of the implications of this! The Heart Sutra essentially says that whenever you feel life is stuck, it's just a concept. It's a mental construct. Therefore, it is malleable, flexible…in other words, changeable. It's not set in stone as much as you think it is. I know earlier I mentioned Pema Chodron's book of how there is no true escape. But now, there is a certain type of "escape," which is changing your mental angle in life!

If you don't believe me, that's fine. But just look at all the people in life who have overcome immense suffering. Did they escape their positions or conditions in life by believing that their situations were 100% solid and set? The answer is obvious: NO. If you look at any great hero who has overcome huge obstacles, they did so because they refused to believe that their current lot was the only reality there was. Nelson Mandela spent over 27 years in physical prison! According to his writings, however, you can see that he was constantly changing his mental angle of what was a prison for himself. This constant emptying out of mental conceptions is what allowed him to not only keep his sanity but ultimately be free, despite the fact that he was in prison!

I have never met Nelson Mandela, but I have worked with prisoners, mostly in the form of teaching them meditation and life skills like the ones in this book. I had the great privilege of working with Fleet Maull[9] when he lived here in Colorado. He is a famous Buddhist, life skills teacher, author, and meditation instructor who spent 14 years in a federal prison! Learning and teaching with him was an extraordinary experience. I always have looked to him as a man who walked the walk in terms of changing the mental angle of life. He embodied an understanding of emptiness for me and always will.

I feel this emptiness, or ability to change your mental angle in life can be expressed in all Jiu Jitsu. In the example of the side control escape, the Change of Angle comes from turning into your opponent. When the defender gets to her or his side, the attacker's weight is dispersed and not as equal on the bottom person. This weakens the attacker's sense of control and allows the defender to succeed to a more advantageous position.

Similarly, you might want to apply the Inner Jiu Jitsu way of Changing your Mental Angle in small ways at first. Start by asking yourself if this mental narrative you are carrying is really true? If your gut says yes, then ask it again with more intensity. Is the thought you're having, the story you're telling yourself exactly true? Are you

---

9   Fleet spent 14 years in a federal penitentiary for drug charges and changed his life while in prison. Learn more about him at: http://fleetmaull.com/

exaggerating even a little? Just entertaining the possibility that your version of reality may not be the only one could be enough to crack the emotional trauma of a situation. Once you get that small opening, the rest of the process becomes easier.

APPLYING BUDDHIST EMPTINESS AND CHANGING THE ANGLE

Have you ever been in a relationship with someone that you cared about but weren't able to bridge some communication problems? Many times in relationships, we find ourselves stuck. We care about the person, but we get stuck in the same old routines and negative habitual patterns. You have two choices: Stay the exact same, which means just silently hope for something better but do nothing of substance to change, which means you will get the same result. OR, be strong, take a challenge and actually turn into the pain of your relationship but with intelligence and strategy.

You might be saying to yourself, "If it's so much pain, why on Earth would someone actually stay the same if it means the same or increased amounts of suffering?" Well, people do this all the time, and the reason is usually this: If you don't do anything, you get to attain certainty in your situation. When people feel certain, they meet a basic need inside themselves. Even if our sense of certainty is warped and negative, it gives us some reassurance that we have a sense of predictability in our lives. This feeling is deep and ultimately makes us "feel" safe. However, if the certainty is based in something horrible or not life enhancing, it's going to take its toll on us ultimately. Lucky for us, there is another path.

So let's take a deep breath, trust in something higher and greater than our usual habits, and take the plunge to try something different.

The fact that you are reading this book is proof that you are willing to do something different.

Now we are going to apply the same wisdom in escaping from side control or slipping the cross into our lives.

Step one: Accept that life has suffering and pain in it.

What? Did I just plagiarize the Buddha's first noble truth? Well, yes. (Except he didn't copyright his material so legally I'm okay. Also, even the Buddha was the first to say that he didn't create a new religion or law of the universe; he only re-discovered it. Therefore, like a physical law of the universe, no one can copyright it because it's a part of nature.) If we can accept that, then the steps to overcome suffering become easy.

There isn't any real escape from **some** of life's suffering. For example, no matter what we do, everyone will die. No matter what we do, there will be people who don't act the way we want them to. It's simply built into the matrix of reality. However, we can make very powerful attitude shifts that will take away some of the *pain* of suffering. This belief shift that life entails suffering, but you can overcome the *pain* of the suffering is tantamount towards success. In fact, it's a rewording of the 3rd Noble Truth.

Come back to being on the bottom of your opponent. This is a perfect metaphor. The opponent might be bigger than you. He might smell, and I don't just mean his gi (not a metaphor for those who roll a lot). The weight can be overwhelming sometimes and if he's good, it can become extremely crushing.

This is life. Life can be crushing. Life can be so demanding, so ruthless, so unforgiving and merciless. However, you can still come out on top. If you can't make it on top, at least you can put yourself in a position where you won't be crushed.

To escape from bottom side mount, a couple of key things need to happen. First, you have to stay centered and believe you can get out. It can happen; you just need a strategy that works. In Jiu Jitsu, it's understanding basic physics and applying biomechanics. In life, it's a metaphysical biomechanics.

If life is crushing you, you have to build up a superior psychology to take you up and out of the situation. That's the starting point. Some of the strategies outlined in Chapter 1 will help you with that. The key is to give it 100% and to practice daily. It's obviously better to have one built up before the horror of a situation crushes you, but you must start where you're at and if today is your first day, SO BE IT. YOU WILL GET OUT. Lesson one then is to accept the suffering of the situation first.

The second step is to CHANGE THE ANGLE. In Jiu Jitsu, this is done by the shrimp movement. Sometimes the movement is so subtle; it's more like a tiny adjustment to get to your side. It may involve a powerful initial UPA, or lift, but then it may be subtle after that.

CHAPTER

8

GETTING A GOOD U.P.A. IN LIFE

U.P.A. - UNIFIED POWER ACTION

THE PHYSICAL UPA is basically a hip bump, usually followed by an immediate hip shift to the side. It's an essential movement that must be practiced over and over. It's used for the entire life of the Jiu Jitsu practitioner from White Belt to Black Belt.

I turned the physical UPA word into Unified Power Action because of the following: A physical UPA unifies and integrates all of your muscles properly for a powerful escape. Similarly, an Inner Jiu Jitsu U.P.A also unites your mind and emotions and (sometimes your body) properly for the most appropriate action.

Here's an example of the power of emotion on the mind. Think about something significant in your life that you actually remember the date for. Perhaps it is the birth of your child, your wedding anniversary, or when a loved one died. Notice how easy it is to recall details about that person or event. You might not remember everything, but certain feelings and images come back very vividly, yes? Now, try to remember what you were doing the day before this significant event. Can you do it with the same amount of clarity? Probably not.

This tiny example shows the psychic imprint that emotions make on the brain. When you add or unify the emotions to the brain, you create a long-lasting impression on the body-mind connection. We know from PTSD sufferers that negative events can ruin lives with vicious effectiveness. If negative events can bring about so much long-lasting suffering, then it stands to reason that positive events can also bring out enduring affirmative effects. Our intention is to build positive life-enhancing impressions that will empower us to carry through when the going gets tough.

The initial U.P.A. could be many things in life, but it comes from inspiration frankly. You could come back from one of my seminars. Or you might be feeling a sense of inspiration from a thousand other possible sources. Books, poems, nature, walking, hiking, a good talk, there are almost too many to mention. When you have a good psychology, everything can be a pathway towards improving and succeeding in life.

In fact, that's why optimists tend to succeed better than realists[10]. When a tragedy comes to an optimist, he or she will see the obstacle as a way to get better on some level. He or she might even see this as divinely ordained and set out to find some powerful meaning out of

---

10   http://www.livescience.com/39128-optimistic-realists-do-best.html

the situation. A realist might see the situation more accurately but might not make the necessary mental adjustments to feel better.

You can see this very succinctly in some people who have undergone something very traumatic like cancer. Cancer, by every standard I can think of, is simply horrible. When you or someone you know gets it, it's an incredibly hard challenge to overcome. Yet there are many who have overcome it, either physically, or mentally, or both. These people take a completely different view of their disease. Some actually think it's one of the greatest things to happen to them because it opens them up to the deepest spectrums of life. Some have claimed that it was actually "given" to them by God to make them a better human being. You might not agree with them theologically, but that kind of mental attitude sure does change their reaction to the disease. Not only that, but the subsequent physical reaction due to their mental shift can become a powerful tool for healing.

It makes sense if you think about it. It's just like in outer Jiu Jitsu when you decide to train when you're feeling like crap, and then you feel like a million bucks after your session. What affects the mind, affects the body, and what affects the body, affects the mind. So if you have a crappy mental state, your body is going to suffer. But if you go in with a great mental state, your performance is going to be way better! So change your mind! Similarly, if you use your body correctly, you can really alter your mental state to one of peak performance!

In Jiu Jitsu, nothing beats a real powerful U.P.A. I personally think that if you want to get one in your own life, attend a powerful seminar or workshop. Yes, they cost money, but because they are so immersive, they really can change your life and mind in a very meaningful and drastic way.

Sometimes, we are gifted by Grace to get a great U.P.A. simply out of the circumstances of life. You get so disgusted with the way things are going that you simply say, "ENOUGH IS ENOUGH" and decide to make big changes in your life. Sometimes, your psychology is already primed to make this kind of change, and you get inspired by something mundane or ordinary. Your son or daughter or teacher says something to you and suddenly, you're no longer the same. Sometimes, a good book or quote touches your soul. I remember when I was 21, I read an inspiring quote from a calendar that just rocked my world. It was the chemist, Marie Curie. It said, "*Nothing is to be feared, only UNDERSTOOD.*" If you're reading this, you too might feel the same power of that quote! It embodies the message of the bottom side control position metaphor.

Once you've changed your mindset and believe you can get out of the pain, you can now proceed to the next step of CHANGING THE ANGLE. This can involve a shrimp or a simple subtle movement to your side in outer Jiu Jitsu, but in Inner Jiu Jitsu, it's changing your perspective on a situation. Making a mental shift is one of the greatest strategies you can employ. All champions in all areas of life use it for success. Never underestimate the power of even a small attitude shift. Even though it may not seem all that dramatic, the effect can be a giant game changer.

Let's look at how a small shift in changing can affect an area of your life. Let's pick one that affects everyone: money. Many want to save money, but they don't believe there is any way for them to do it. Ironically, many people also believe they must have the latest greatest phone the moment it comes out. There simply is no scientific proof that either is true. If you can challenge that thought that a new phone will somehow enhance your life, you're applying an *Angle Shift* in your mind.

Let's look at the phone problem a little further. I feel that most phone companies are crooks that are out to rip you off. They talk a lot of fluff by promising you all the latest features and a "discounted" phone. What most people don't realize is that each time you hear of a "free" or discounted state of the art phone with a two-year contract is that you'll be paying far more than buying a slightly less than super modern phone upright and paying for the service charges. Let's do some simple math here:

Sprint/Verizon/T-Mobile/AT&T have a deal where you can have the latest phone iPhone or otherwise for $200 or less. You simply pay for the service of the company and that can run anywhere from $80-120 for a single line. Yes, they might say it only costs $50 or $60, but then they hit you with tons of hidden fees which will add on to at least $20-$26 extra, which may or may not include phone insurance. Over the course of your two-year contract at a meager 80 dollars, you will have spent at least $2100.

Now compare this with a plan from say Virgin Mobile or Metro PC. Here, you usually pay for the phone outright. Yes, you might have to pay several hundred dollars for a new iPhone or Samsung if you're going for the latest model. However, once you're paid for the phone, you pay a much smaller monthly fee. Last time I used Virgin Mobile, I paid almost $37 exactly including taxes for an iPhone with unlimited data. (They took $5 off my monthly bill for signing up for automatic debit). The cost for 2 years worth of owning the phone came to a total of $888. Compare that with the $2100 mentioned earlier. Even if you include the total phone cost of approximately $600, you're only paying a total of $1488. This alone will save you at least $600 over two years. Another plus is since you own the phone completely now, you can decide to sell it when you want. I sold my old iPhone 4s for $200 bucks on eBay. In the end, you're going to be saving anywhere from $600-800 in the course of two years. In addition, you'll be paying less per month. Who knows what you could do with that extra income of $50? Perhaps more Jiu Jitsu lessons, or your 401K, or a stock investment.

As you can see, sometimes all it takes to achieve an Angel Shift is to think something through, and you will come up with a solution. Never underestimate your own problem-solving ability.

To achieve the Angle Shifts in life, you have to take on a strategy and apply it diligently and continuously. You can't be haphazard and apply your techniques or new psychology when it's convenient. It has to be a consistent force and habit in your life. Again, any of the aforementioned techniques in Mastering the Space of your Mind section could constitute great U.P.A.'s if you use them consistently every day.

So let's go back to the relationship that you're in. If there were 3 Levels that you could rate your relationship in right now, where would you put it? Level 1 represents a really crappy relationship. If you're at this level, hang tight because we do have a solution for that, but it doesn't happen until the next section.

Level 2 represents where a large majority of us are at. We are in a relationship that is sweet at times but could definitely be better. We care for this person a lot, but we also feel that there are some serious communication issues, and/or we don't receive the total amount of joy or happiness we expect from this person. Maybe we feel we are simply in a rut. If this is the case, you have to apply the Angle Shift in a way that turns into your opponent and NOT run away or in Jiu Jitsu talk, "gives up your back."

Level 3 represents a fantastic relationship so we won't spend time on it in this book (but maybe in volume 2.)

Moving into your opponent is moving into your fear, your

pain, your obstacle, but with intelligence and strategy. If this is a relationship issue and you're at Stage 2, then it's essentially saying you value the relationship more than the fear and problems you're currently having. If it's a job, then it's saying that you like your job but you want something more from it. You can apply this principle to anything you're having a Stage 2 feeling with. It basically comes down to this question: Do I value this thing more than the pain and suffering it entails? In other words, is this worth it? If you can honestly say yes, then you are in a Stage 2 dilemma, and you need to attack with a Stage 2 Inner Jiu Jitsu strategy.

STAGE 2 PSYCHOLOGY OF MOVING INTO YOUR FEAR

To achieve success with a Stage 2 psychology, you need to look yourself in the mirror, and say to yourself: THIS IS WORTH FIGHTING FOR. I DON'T WANT TO GIVE UP. This is a powerful moment, and it's very important to actually use your physical voice and say those things out loud. If you are struggling with just saying it, then SCREAM IT. If you are doing it by yourself, you have absolutely nothing to fear or get embarrassed about, so just do it!

Do it more than once, do it 3 to 30 times. Let each successive statement increase in power. Get physical! Engage your body and face muscles. The physical movements can release powerful chemicals for change. Let your mind and body go and embrace your statement that you are going to GO FOR IT! Do it whenever you're feeling down and you doubt yourself. Have fun with it but also say it seriously. Doubt and uncertainty are awful feelings. The only antidote is the certainty that you're going to fight for the thing you value. This is your U.P.A. This technique sets your mind up for success.

Now, the second technique is using a great strategy. The escape from bottom side control is about staying calm in adversity, getting to your side, and putting yourself in a position of greater power. It rests on changing yourself, not the other person. When you get to your side, the opponent's weight gets slightly disrupted and it allows you greater mobility. This is an incredible exercise in leverage and you can use the same metaphor for any of your challenges.

Strategy number 1. Write down a Mission Statement

This is so simple, yet so powerful. It is an extension of our Voice. It rests on the same principle of using your Inner and Outer Voice. Essentially it stems from the power of the Word (Vak in Sanskrit). Make a Poster or at the very least get a journal and write down your commitment to your relationship or your job, or whatever it is you're seeking to change. Write down the specifics of what you want to accomplish. Just like in Jiu Jitsu, you don't initially try to push or manipulate your opponent. You make changes to yourself to make a difference to the opponent. Similarly, if you want your environment, relationship, or work conditions to change you must start with yourself. Make your goals specific and clear. Avoid ambiguity at all costs. Instead of making a goal like "I want more money next year," be specific and write, "I will make an extra $2500 dollars next year."

Figure 19: In order to enact change, you work on yourself first. Master Luiz Claudio, Rickson Gracie Black Belt, illustrates this.

Figure 20: Notice the change Professor Luiz performs on himself to set up the potential change in the opponent. Similarly, you have to start changing your own psychology first before you can change life circumstances. You are directly connected to the universe of cause and effect.

Making a poster can actually be a lot of fun. It's like being in grade school again. You can get as imaginative as you want. You can cut out magazine pictures out, or print images from the internet. You want to make this fun and creative. The more effort and creativity you put into it, the more you will value it. It will be like anything you decide to accessorize. If you accessorize your Jiu Jitsu gi, for example, it becomes more valuable and enjoyable to you. So have fun with it.

Having your poster someplace where you will see it every day will be paramount to your success. It should be inspiring. You want to see this at least twice a day. My vision poster is in the hallway to my home. It's the last thing I see when I leave for the day, and the first thing I see when I get home.

Strategy 2: Journal Work Is Like Having A Great Gameplan

In addition to making a Vision Poster, it is equally important to journal and **WRITE** down what you want to accomplish. The act of physically writing is paramount. I don't know why, but something happens to the brain when you take a pen or pencil and put your thoughts on paper. I suppose a computer can work as well, but from the studies I've seen, paper and pencil seem to have the highest impact[11]. If you think about it, this is an aspect of our evolutionary progress as human beings. You might as well take advantage of this trait. From a spiritual point of view, it seems to extend the principles of the power of our inner Divinity. As I stated before, it's another

---

11 http://lifehacker.com/5738093/why-you-learn-more-effectively-by-writing-than-typing

extension of the principles of VAK or speech, since writing is a form of language.

Journal work is an ongoing process. It's something that has to happen at least twice a week. You don't want to let a great idea, goal, or problem you're processing to go too long without journal work. The great thing about it is that it's easy. You're just writing down and processing your thoughts and ideas. One of the essential teachings of many systems of spirituality is that YOU ARE IT (Tat vam asi in Sanskrit, a common teaching in the Upanishads). YOU ARE THE ULTIMATE SOURCE. YOU ARE THE BADASS. YOU ARE THE KNOWLEDGE YOU SEEK. A lot of times, your IT-ness is in a potential state, waiting to unleash. Hopefully, this book is helping to unlock some of your potential.

Just as practicing outer Jiu Jitsu is one of the best physical martial arts you can practice, doing journal work is one of the best things a human being can do for oneself. However, you shouldn't always write in your journal as a "stream of consciousness" style. Although that can be helpful and certainly needed at times, you need to write with a sense of purpose. Therefore, if there is something that is bothering you, or you are seeking some change in your life, PROCESS IT BY WRITING IT DOWN. I guarantee you, if you do proper journal work on your goals in life for 15 minutes a day, your higher SELF will come up with a number of solutions you never thought possible.

Your writing is an extension of your life. You want to write with INTENTION and PURPOSE. If you are struggling with a business decision, a major project, or a romantic relationship, write about it. Go through your feelings, what you truly want out of it, and what you are willing to do to make changes on your end. The same goes for a bad work relationship. Write down all your wants and desires from your job, and what you are willing to do on your side to make it happen. The same goes for greater financial independence. What are your feelings about your current situation? What do you truly want? What are you willing to change about yourself to accomplish your dreams?

Strategy 3: Applying Journal Work Is Just Like Applying Good Pressure

Like the side bottom mount escape, the last part is crucial. You can have a great UPA and get to your side, but if you don't make the final re-entry with your knee and elbow and establish the Guard position, you will still be stuck in a bad position with a lot of weight and potential damage to rain upon you AGAIN.

Here are the THREE GOLDEN questions you should always ask yourself before starting your journal work.

1. **What do I want**? Be specific and clear

2. **Why do I want it?**

3. **What am I going to do to accomplish it?**

The last question should actually be divided into two parts. You can either make two columns or just leave lots of space for each subdivision. One column is for your general plan, the other will be for absolute MUST DO specific action items to make the plan a reality.

What is painful about not getting what you want? Write down everything you can. What is positive or healthy or game changing if you attain what you want? One of three things will happen then from this.

1. You're going to associate pain and suffering and want to avoid it by changing your life. 2. You're going to associate more positivity

with your change. 3. You're going to do both in a synergistic way and use the pain and pleasure appropriately.

This process of writing it down consistently creates change. When you see the pain that you are creating by not engaging in what you really want, it will drive you to pursue your goals harder. But so will the pleasure of realizing you are going to attain your goal. It's no different than training hard in outer Jiu Jitsu drills. You experience pain, but it's temporary, and it's worth the pleasure of becoming a better Jiu Jitsu practitioner. This is one simple way that can create the little shifts you need to change or "get in a better position" from a Jiu Jitsu point of view. What works on the ground, works in life.

WHAT TO DO IF YOU ARE IN A STAGE 1 RELATIONSHIP OR SITUATION

In this stage, there are only two things to do. You either upgrade the relationship (and by that you hope the person goes up with you), or you get out. There really is no gray area here.

Upgrading the relationship is very difficult because it really depends on the other person evolving with you. It is sometimes hard to predict if the person will actually help themselves and want to be with you in your higher state. It's certainly worth the try if you value the relationship. If this is the case, you offer the same techniques you are using for yourself, and hopefully, your partner will like your change and join you. That would be the best. You want a partner to share the path with.

However, if your personal or professional relationship is really stifling, and you've tried everything you could and it still stinks, then you have to abandon your current life situation. Even if it means, "giving up your back", you have to do it at this point. Look at the following techniques and see if you can see the metaphor.

Figure 21: This escape series represents the need of just getting the hell out of a bad situation. It comes when you've tried as much as you can, yet your life situation simply is not enriching you the way you would like. It's time to move on and get out. You may lose an arm in the process!

As effective as the aforementioned technique is, however, the following one gives the defender a complete victory. Enjoy!

Figure 22: The key to this move is to "bait" and "trap" your opponent's arm by opening your arm so much that he will want to instinctively wrap around your waist. Unlike the previous escape, your arm will not be arm-barred because it is so high up. This is a metaphor of taking the smart path of getting out of a bad situation in life but with style, skill, and intelligence.

Figure 23: In this particular case, you whip your opponent on his back and complete your victory with an arm-bar of your own. This shows that with the right psychology and strategy, you can be victorious in all aspects of your life!

In both of these techniques, the physical expression of "getting the hell out even at the expense of giving up your back" is apparent. If you do it with skill, however, you can still walk away victorious. Usually, in outer Jiu Jitsu we don't like to expose the back ever. However, in dire situations like the ones we mention, you might have to really go for broke. These techniques and the subsequent metaphor are obviously saved for when things in your life really are crappy. You have to do it, however. You can't mess around. The good news is this is done with intelligence and a sense of strategy so you're not just flopping around and wasting energy while not getting anywhere closer to escape.

Visualization of "Escaping and exposing the back" metaphor

Imagine your life in this crappy state, position, or relationship whether it's an intimate relationship or job relationship, five years from now. How does it make you feel? If you are feeling a sense of vomit, nausea, deep uncertainty, or regret, you need to apply a Stage 1 psychological escape technique. You must summon up the feelings of regret and disgust you have and use it to fuel your escape. You must get out! You must imagine with every sense you have living this substandard way of life and dying with it. Visualize yourself on your deathbed with your child or loved ones near you, hearing and watching you die as you breathe your last breath. Feel the sense of life altering regret and loss as you start to die, knowing that you lived a life only partially fulfilled. What do you say to yourself and your loved ones at this moment? Can you honestly look them in the eyes and say that you lived your life to the fullest? Or is your heart filled with misery as you look at them and try to rationalize your life of unfulfilled dreams? To make this even more powerful, take 3 powerful breaths and then hold it on the last one as you go through your visualization of dying unfulfilled. Hold it as long as you can while you go through the scenarios of living this life of regret. *You must imagine this is how you will die!* Imagine this as your last breath. When you cannot hold your breath any longer, take a deep inhalation and start to slowly breathe again. You should hopefully feel some gratitude that you didn't die and have the chance to change your life the way you want to.

This vision should frighten you, to the point where you're crying. You can't take visualizations lightly. When you hear the word "imagine" you have to try your absolute hardest to actively "imagine" and feel the scenario at hand.

It's no different than visualizing prior to a tournament. You use all your senses and at the very least, try to "feel" your vision. The ideal situation is to do both; imagine and feel your visualization. Use the fuel of pain and suffering to get you out of your current situation. Let it drive you. In outer Jiu Jitsu, you do these more risky techniques when you absolutely must get out, meaning the weight of the guy is unbearable, or you're down on points and the clock is running and you're going to lose if you do nothing. Certainly, the metaphor of these techniques is evident. GET OUT. Use this technique and escape to a new life.

Another way to "get out" of this bad position is to change your overall attitude of how things should be. There is a pretty surefire way to formulate suffering and pain in life. It goes like this: Have a certain expectation of how you think life should be, and then wait until life isn't the way you expect it and watch and feel the suffering arise. The equation looks something like this:

Life expectations + Unmatched Reality = Suffering

One way to change this equation to a positive is to change your life expectations. Again, change your Angle like you would in Outer Jiu Jitsu to get out of a bad position! Your angle is your perception in life! Are your expectations and attitude of how things should be unaligned with reality?

Sometimes, for example, it's practical to keep a certain job for a time period because it's secure and pays the bills, even though you hate it. If you can accept it as a temporary position, and hold on to a goal that you're using it as a stepping stone to better things, that may be an intelligent and great strategy!

It's more like the second technique now, which looks dangerous and risky but it's done with a higher goal of winning. There were jobs I hated but helped me towards certain benefits because I kept my mind focused on the future when I would be in a better spot and could strike off. I changed my mental angle on the situation and questioned if this job really was as bad as I thought. I questioned the practicality of leaving since it would cause more harm than good. In the end, I did leave that position, but only once I was certain I had a much better one and achieved a greater level of happiness. It took three years in my case. The point is by changing my life expectations, I changed the equation. In fact, you could rewrite the formula this way:

Reality (life conditions) + life expectations= happiness.

I think everyone should go for their dreams to the fullest. But you do have to have patience. As Oprah once said, "You can have it all, just not all at once." Be smart about things. If things really are as bad as you think they are, then, by all means, get the hell out and find something new. But sometimes, we can work with what we have for the time being.

It's just like good Jiu Jitsu players who thrive on the bottom. They hone their skills as a counter fighter, guard player, or even bad position player. If you watch the match of Javier Vasquez versus Garry Tonon, it's like they don't even care that they get put in bad positions because they are very comfortable there. I would put Jeff Glover in that camp as well. See if you can apply those champion styles to your Inner Jiu Jitsu.

Summary for obtaining a great U.P.A. in life:

1. *Allow* some grace or inspiration to take a hold of you for something you want in life.

2. Utilize all emotions to get your emotional momentum going including the all important visualization of death meditation. Use physical exercise to get your mental juices running as well.

3. Apply good journal work by writing down a mission statement and the Three Golden Questions:
   - What do I want? (BE PRECISE)
   - Why do I want it? (BE SPECIFIC)
   - What will I do to get it? (BE ACCURATE)

4. Keep the belief that you are the greatness you seek and always seek the best strategy to obtain your desired outcomes! Continue to use visualizations to play the long game for continued growth!

CHANGING THE ANGLE IN REGARDS TO LUCID DREAMING

SINCE CHANGING THE Angle in Inner Jiu Jitsu is really describing the mind's ability to change its position in terms of belief, and therefore its version of reality, you can use it for anything. This includes lucid dreaming.

One of the first steps towards lucid dreaming is to constantly question your sense of reality. You do this by just asking yourself throughout different points of the day whether what you're experiencing is "real" or not. So let's say you stop reading and go to your refrigerator and get a snack. Pause and ask yourself, "Is this real? Am I dreaming?" Go back to this book and read some more. If you can remember to ask yourself at least three times throughout the day whether what you're doing is real, or part of a dream, you're on your way to starting to crack the "solidness" of reality.

These small cracks start to open up to more possibilities in life. It starts with some silly, almost superficial questioning a couple times a day. But after awhile, you increase the quantitative moments of questioning and also increase the amount of emotional intensity in which you ask it. Truly ask yourself, "Is this REAL? Am I DREAMING?" Those two questions might open similar lines of questioning reality.

With enough questioning, a night is going to come when your conscious mind has been trained so well to question reality during waking hours that the same line of thinking is going to permeate your dream consciousness. At this point, you'll be dreaming about whatever big or small, silly or horrifying, adventure and then the question will come out of you, "Is this REAL? AM I DREAMING?" in the middle of your dream! You'll question your version of reality and maybe, just maybe, you'll wake up in your dream but still be dreaming. When this happens, you become invincible and fearless because there is a recognition of whatever you're experiencing or observing is all coming from your consciousness. Talk about non-duality! Your obstacles were completely made up by your own mind.

As you can see, Changing the Mental Angle and applying Inner Jiu Jitsu has some broad implications. If outer Jiu Jitsu can take you out of terrifying life-threatening positions, then Inner Jiu Jitsu should be able to save you from mental threatening conditions as well. Hopefully, it will save you even in threatening dream conditions also!

Neuroplasticity is all the rage right now, mainly because it merges cutting edge science with some age-old spiritual intuitions. Applying Angle Shifts from Inner Jiu Jitsu is plasticity in action. It's one wonderful application of the "Jiu" aspect of Jiu Jitsu. Inner Jiu Jitsu is essentially asking us to not take ourselves so seriously over and over again so that our sense of reality becomes more flexible. The character of "Jiu" usually connotes softness or flexibility when hardship comes your way. One aspect is yielding to force. However, the higher aspect relates to harmony with our obstacles, and that can happen when we "soften" our grip on reality.

SENSITIVITY AND CONNECTION: THE ULTIMATE TRAIT

THIS CHAPTER MIGHT be the deepest one in the book, philosophically speaking.

If you are a Jiu Jitsu player, do you know what the number one attribute that makes a black belt master different than the rest? If you can't guess, then I'll tell you:

SENSITIVITY

Think about the last time you lost to someone you looked up to in Jiu Jitsu. Assuming it wasn't because they were manhandling you because they possessed an inhuman strength or crushing you with tons of weight, the real reason a master defeats you time and time again is because he or she has heightened his or her awareness of sensitivity.

Personally speaking, I am always amazed when I am beaten by my opponent not because of his size or strength, and not because of some crazy outlandish move, but by the simple arm bar, or sweep, or choke, that I know too, but can't defend against. I know you're familiar with this feeling. One question burns in your mind: "*How did they do that?*"

The reason they can pull that off and we can't is because they have developed their *myelin sheaths*[12] so much that they feel our reactions and respond appropriately before we can respond. Why can Roger Gracie pull off the simplest white belt arm bars, chokes, and sweeps on some of the best champions in the game? It's the same move we've all been taught. What makes Roger special is that he feels the opponent more and reacts off their reaction. He doesn't just muscle through. He is so sensitive to his opponent's micro movements that he reacts to them in a way that is seamless and makes him one or two steps ahead of his opponent. In this sense, he *becomes one* with his adversary.

When described in this manner, the art of Jiu Jitsu becomes a teaching in non-duality. The master becomes so attuned to their opponent, that the idealized state of "oneness" is temporarily achieved. What are you one with? *Your opponent.* If the opponent moves, you move. If he pushes, you pull. If he pulls, you push. If

---

12 The myelin sheath is essentially the layer on a nerve cell. The more formed the layer becomes, the higher and faster it functions. In essence, the more you practice any skill, the more myelin sheath you create. Those who are masters have developed thick myelin sheaths. https://www.ncbi.nlm.nih.gov/books/NBK27954/

you're trying to sweep him, you make a certain pressure and wait for the appropriate reaction. Once he reacts, your counter attack becomes perfected and you achieve the submission or sweep. It happens sometimes in huge overt ways, but it can also happen in small micro adjustments.

I had the opportunity to take a seminar with Roger Gracie once. He showed all of us exactly how to set up his famous collar choke from a sweep. It was a move I learned when I was a white belt, so I wondered why he was bothering with it. *The "ah-ha" moment hit when he mentioned how you wait for the reaction of the opponent.* If you try to hit the sweep when all his weight is on you, you'll be depending on your strength to overcome his weight. However, if you set up one extra movement and then bait him to adjust, the sweep becomes easier to execute. He did this exact move later in a match against world champion Rodrigo Medeiros:

Figure 24: A typical Flower Sweep technique. What the skilled player does though is hard to see. The advanced player waits to feel the top person's weight shift. That's when you initiate the off balancing and create a momentum shift with the leg in the armpit.

Figure 25: It's this tiny shift that makes all the difference. The opponent cannot just sit there. He must move to adjust for his own escape. When you feel his hips leave his feet is when you add momentum and continue the off balancing process. <u>Similarly, in life, it is the sensitivity to stay connected to your true goals that keep you grounded in what you want and need</u>.

This attention to the smallest detail of micro adjustments to your opponent must become cultivated in your life if you want victory both on and off the mat. If you can become more aware and sensitive to your opponent, your chances of victory and ultimate mastery will improve drastically. Take the challenge, become the master!

APPLICATION OF SENSITIVITY

Non-duality and sensitivity are often esoteric subjects, and therefore not easy to teach. However, that should never stop one from seeking it. It's usually easier than one thinks. It's in the subtleness that we "miss" it. This chapter is essentially an attempt to link something very subtle and profound like non-duality with a concept in martial arts known as *sensitivity*. I chose the concept of sensitivity because it's in sensitivity exercises that we sometimes "merge" with our opponent and therefore gain the upper hand. We stay connected to them and feel even their micro movements. Take that idea of staying connected to your opponent and now apply it to divine nature.

Being sensitive essentially means being aware of your own highest nature and following that instead of your egotistic superficial mind wanderings. The first couple lines from the Yoga Sutras of Patanjali come to mind in this regards.

Yoga Sutra 1: Now is the Study of Union with the Ultimate Essence.

Yoga Sutra 2: To become One with the Essence of one's Consciousness, the student must stop identifying with the active fluctuating thoughts of the mind.

Yoga Sutra 3: When that is achieved, then the true greatness of the practitioner shines forth!

Yoga Sutra 4: Otherwise, the practitioner will identify with the mind's superficial thoughts.

(A loose translation rendered by yours truly).

Here's my application of how to use and apply sensitivity and become more "one" with all aspects of your life:

1. Think about the goals you have. (This is rooted in the *Essence*)

2. Now think about what is the feeling behind all of your desires for those goals. For example, if you have a goal for a better relationship with your wife, *focus on the feeling* you associate with achieving that dream. If you want to become more wealthy, focus on the *feeling* you would have of being wealthy.

3. When you focus on that feeling of achieving your goals, be sure to keep your eyes on the REAL prize. Money, for example, is just paper. It's not that special in and of itself. It's a material thing that is essentially the same material as toilet paper, something you wipe your ass with. An infant or toddler might eat money because he or she doesn't associate any type of value for it. Yet, even a toddler can respond to the *feeling* that a mother or father can offer the child. The same goes for relationships. When you want to reconcile with a spouse or girlfriend, you're looking for a *feeling* to be restored. If you're in an argument or conflict with a business or work partner, focus on the *feeling* you want from achieving what you want with them. (But try and leave revenge out of it!) This is how I interpret the third line of the Yoga Sutras. The practitioner focuses on the essence nature of the soul, which is more of a *feeling* than a thought.

4. If you can be more attuned to the ***feeling*** of attaining your goals, then you're becoming much closer to actualizing sensitivity in your life. Why? Because you are training the parts of your soul that are in tune with your greater needs and not your superficial thoughts. Feelings are your greater needs! We desire certain feelings no matter what our age, gender, or status. If we focus on actions, thoughts, or results that are not grounded in the feelings behind those actions, then we get bogged down and distracted by that which will not help us. This is what I mean by the fourth line in the Yoga Sutras. If you don't focus on the true goal you desire, the true feeling, you will get caught up in a non-essential thought. When that happens, you will identify with that and stray from the path!

In other words, always focus on the overall outcome you want in your interactions with others. If you're arguing with your wife, focus on the greater desire of feeling loved and at peace rather than trying to prove you're right. If you are in an argument with a co-worker, focus on the feeling of achieving a positive outcome that you want. (**Do your best to avoid trying to prove someone wrong or yourself right**. Unless you're a lawyer, trying to prove you're right all the time is a misinformed goal and keeps your eyes off the submission, or target. It is a very common mistake). That's keeping your eyes on the real prize.

Focusing on this will keep you on what really benefit you. In the end, you're always desiring and needing a **feeling** more than a perception or idea. Sensitivity is being aware by the act of feeling. Be sensitive to the overall outcomes you seek in life, not your ego's idea of what it thinks is right. When you do this, your sense of overwhelm will diminish because you'll be focusing on what you ultimately want in life's circumstances and not the everyday wear and tear of things to do. This will motivate you.

In other words, focus on your desired outcome! What do you really want? How you answer this will drive your focus! What you focus on becomes the bullseye for all your energy. If you put your focus on the right targets, life will be a breeze. If you allow it to drag you in superficial directions, it'll distract you away from what really serves you. It's no different in outer Jiu Jitsu. If you're competing in a sports Jiu Jitsu competition, your ultimate goal is to win. That's where your focus should be, and that is your bullseye target. If it's a submission only tournament, your goal is to submit or at the very least, not be submitted. Each tournament has different goals with different effects. Let's use this idea in terms of time management.

CHAPTER 11

GETTING THE SUBMISSION IN TERMS OF TIME MANAGEMENT

L ET'S SAY YOU are a busy parent who feels overwhelmed with all your responsibilities as a mom or dad. You really want to connect with your child, but your responsibilities are driving you crazy. The few moments you do have with your child are spent in a stressed out state. So when you go to sleep at night, even though all you want is to connect with your child, you're driving your child away because the little time spent with them is ruined, and you go to sleep day in and day out feeling dejected and defeated. Let's use the lesson of connection and sensitivity of Inner Jiu Jitsu to change things around.

First, start again with your **ultimate goal or outcome** for a particular situation. In this case, let's assume it's connecting with your child on the deepest level and **feeling** that relationship grow in a healthy loving way. That part is easy. Now, think about your "to do" lists that get in the way of you connecting with your child. Your intention is to bond with your kid but you feel like there are all these responsibilities that get in the way. You have to drive the kids to and fro, pick up groceries, prepare dinner, maintain your job at work, pay the bills, complete projects with deadlines and still go to Jiu Jitsu practice! In addition, you might have a side job that brings you fulfillment, but now you don't have the time or energy to perform well in that. This to-do list is really distracting you from your overall goal and you feel hopeless.

Put the overall outcome you want in the center and put all the to-do's on the outer parts. It should look something like this:

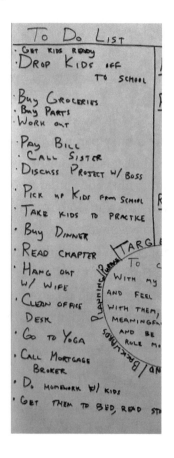

As you look at your "*to-do*" list, notice how you feel. Do you feel worried, stressed, shame, guilt, anxiety, or just plain frantic? Observe your feelings, but stay with me. We're going to bust through.

If we categorize our techniques, we can categorize our "to-do's"

When studying Jiu Jitsu, we have specific categorizations of techniques. Sometimes a teacher will spend an entire class on just arm bars, or escapes from the back, or gi chokes. We can apply this idea of *categorizing* with our "to-do" list as well.

If we look at all the "to-do's" we listed, can we identify certain items that could be considered part of the same category? For example, do you notice three or four activities that relate to health and fitness? Do you notice three or four maybe are related to money or finances? Are there some on your list that are geared towards your career? Relationships? Write down some of these category names on the space to the top right. You can fill in the exact items under the correct heading now.

When you're done, take a look. How does it feel? First, your "to do's" are organized so you might feel less stressed. Second, if you focus on just your new categories, you might feel less overwhelmed because instead of twenty things to do, you have only five:

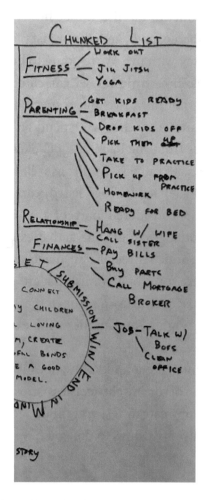

Figure 26: This is the right side of the paper. The giant list from before has been categorized into chunks or sections.

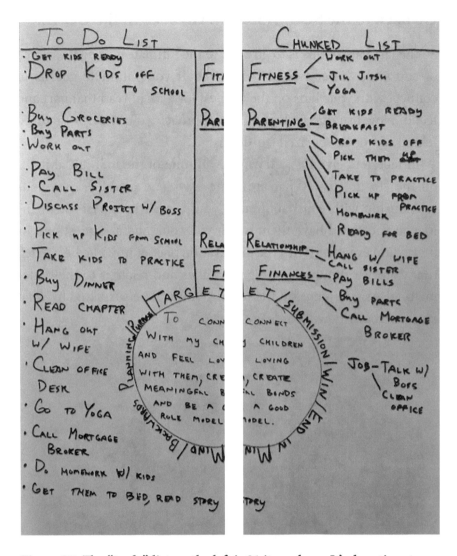

Figure 27- The "to-do" list on the left is 21 items long. It's daunting, to say the least. The new "chunked list" on the right is only 5 items long: 1. Fitness 2. Parenting 3. Relationships 4. Finances 5. Job.

Go back to the SUBMISSION! Go back to the GOAL!

So the last part of this is to go back to the ultimate goal again, which of course is the end result you want. If your ultimate goal is to connect with your kids on the deepest level, then read that part and feel it. Now use that **feeling** as you approach your newly organized "chunked," or categorized "to-do" list.

In fact, let's give this a try now with one of the first initial items on the "to do" list. What are some ways you could deepen your relationship with your children as you prepare breakfast for them? Maybe you could have them watch you cook and ask questions, or they could even help with the preparation of cooking. Maybe you tell funny stories about exploding volcanoes and relate it to the butter melting! As you focus on the feeling, you will be surprised by what kind of creativity will come out of you.

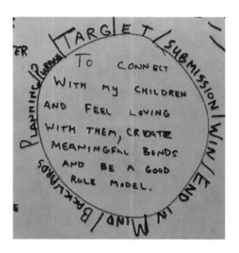

Figure 28- The "Submission" is your ultimate goal!

This process needs to be done for the other activities as well. Since there is a steady amount of times where you are dropping off and picking up, perhaps we can see opportunities there for connecting with our children. Maybe when they get in the car, you have an audio book they like to hear and you talk to them about it. Maybe you turn off the stereo completely and listen and tell stories to each other.

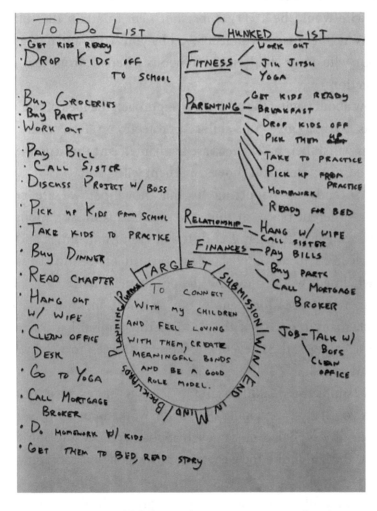

Figure 29 A real life list with Inner Jiu Jitsu application

But what about the tasks not directly related to the little ones? How can hanging out with the wife, or paying bills, deepen our connection with our children? That's easy: you come back to your true goal, your target submission.

If connecting with your children on a deep level is your goal, then it stands to reason that strengthening your relationship with your wife would be a *very important item* to attain that ultimate goal. Why? Because, if you feel loved by your wife, and express love to your wife, your children will obviously benefit from that loving connection.

How about paying the bills? If you approach the idea of paying the bills as a way to give your children protection, safety, security, and certainty that their basic needs are being met, isn't that a great way of being a great parent and showering them with love?

What ends up happening is that now that we are coming from a different place, in this case, the end game, or submission target, we will ultimately *feel* different about our duties and tasks that we need to accomplish. Now instead of feeling stressed or overwhelmed, we feel joy and delight at the chance to get closer to our real target, deepening our connection with our child. In fact, many report that they add to their initial list of "to-do's" because it gives them even *more* opportunities to achieve their ultimate goals.

This simple but real life example needs to be repeated for all the things you truly care about. Do this for your financial goals. Do it for your fitness goals. You can even apply this process to spirituality. In fact, that might be the easiest one to which you can apply these lessons.

The mindfulness movement does a great job of explaining that every moment can be a moment of meditation, or being mindful. So many people will say, "I don't have time to meditate." Maybe they are thinking of sitting meditation, in which case I would say to them, "*Make time to sit*". But if you seriously want to meditate more, just be more mindful in your everyday actions, like talking, brushing your teeth, walking, and even using the bathroom!

Seriously, just observe your thoughts and feelings without reacting and you'll be doing mindfulness. If one of your ultimate goals is to deepen your sense of the divine, then these are some easy and simple ways you can enhance that feeling. Once again, you'll be applying *seiryoku zenyo* every time you attempt this because you'll be increasing your overall efficiency and maximizing your energy.

THE IMPORTANCE OF RENAMING YOUR ROLES

Another easy trick that will help you attack your goals with a sense of vigor and energy is to rename your role in each of your goals. When you do that, you are changing the way you approach it with a new label that instills a feeling of fun and creativity. Take a look back at the category of finances on the previous figure 20. What do you call yourself when you think about your role as a financier? Do you call yourself something boring like "payer of the bills?" How does that name make you feel? Do you feel inspired? Probably not. What if you called yourself something hot and spicy like, "Chief Engineer and Designer of Family Resources?" Or the "Money Lord", or "Bank of Badass"? Do these names bring out a sense of fun and excitement that's better than "payer of bills? It's amazing what a little renaming of your roles will do towards your approach to fulfilling your duties. Take some time and have fun renaming all of your roles. Here are some samples:

Fitness	Parenting	Relationships	Job
Lord Sexy Ass	Lord of the Family	The Fond Father	The Creative Genius
Jiu Jitsu Warrior	Master of the House	The Love Giver	The Powerhouse Player
Master Abs	The Grand Architect	The Sex Sensei	The Skilled Staffer
Ultimate Warrior	The Delightful Dad	Lord of Love	The Hired Hardman

As simple and silly as this is, it helps us *Change our Angle* again towards the mundane and repetitive things we have to do in life. When you rename things, you change your meaning towards it. This is what all UFC fighters and some professional Jiu Jitsu fighters do before they come out to the ring. It makes them feel bigger and grander than some boring and ordinary title. It also brings out wanted attributes and traits in the practitioner that would best serve him. At the very least, it brings out a laugh or smile when you think about your new name and that simple characteristic might lower your negative attitude or stress on the subject.

Fighters who use titles are not the only ones who use the technology of renaming. If you recall the teachings of Vak from the Statements of Power section, the Word has power in life. You may have heard the saying that "Words have meanings". It's true on every level. A good politician knows the power of words affecting his or her followers and pays careful attention to the precise use of words and naming things. When you master the power of language and words, you master aspects of the mind you never thought possible. The power of influencing yourself and others depends largely on how you name and word things.

EXERCISE IN STAYING CONNECTED

It's so important to stay connected to your opponent in outer Jiu Jitsu. When he moves, you move. When he pulls you push. When he pushes you pull. Here's a little meditation exercise to keep you connected to your goals.

Visualize and FEEL whatever it is you desire. Get so sensitive to the feeling that your body responds to it. Walk as if you have your desire. If it's more money, imagine what it would be like to have more than twice the amount of money you have currently. If you want a relationship, imagine what it would be like to have the person of your dreams. How do you stand now? How would the tone of your speech be? How does your body feel? Get so sensitive and really feel it in your body!

Imagine your goal or desire getting brighter and filled with light! Feel it! Maybe you've always wanted to win against a certain opponent. Imagine achieving victory. Take that sense of imaginative freedom and apply it to any aspect of life that you want. How does that feel? Can you literally taste it?

Make it brighter and brighter. Now make it close. Make it so close that instead of just "visualizing" and seeing it, you are becoming it. Take it into your heart! Literally, take the vision and put it right into your heart center. One way is imagine placing your goal or vision directly into your heart. Another way is to imagine the goal being "eaten" so that it does directly go into you (This is my version of "getting **connected** to your essence nature" via Yoga Sutra 3).

After really feeling this, you should notice a change in your body chemistry. Congratulations then! You've just discovered the power of the mind to change the body. Let's do another one.

Go back to your visualization and feeling of your dream, desire, overall goal, or outcome. Now take the feeling and put it in front of you. Be distant from it. Separate yourself from your goal. Watch it from a distance and watch it grow farther and farther away from you. See it get darker and darker and lose its original brightness. Make it so far away and so dark that you can barely connect with it at all.

Now ask yourself: which exercise feels better? If you did this with real effort, the answer should be obvious.

There is no way that you should end this section on a dark note. Go through the first guided meditation one more time and make it brighter than before. In your mind's eye, imagine taking the goal or feeling of the goal and placing it directly in your heart center. BECOME THE GOAL. Actualize the feeling in your heart!! How does that feel?

Use this exercise at least 3 times a week to keep you focused on all of your goals. It will change the way you organize and plan your life. Why? Because you'll be focused on what you truly want.

Feelings are powerful. They can drive countries to war, and they can also bring people to love. Always focus on your feelings and you can accomplish anything. WHY? Because feelings are connected to your heart. If you can really distinguish essence-type feelings from superficial egotistical thoughts, the path for success becomes that much higher because you're connected to a higher sense of self within you.

"If you do not consider to a certain extent whether to put greater emphasis on intellect or emotions, and if you have no clear aim, you cannot practice true seiryoku zenyo. You must first set a goal and apply your energy efficiently. Then educational methods will become clear from the outset, as will the path each individual must follow.

"We must therefore study a method that can be implemented effectively by all citizens in their daily lives and promote its implementation-this is the most urgent task facing us today. That method is, namely, the principle taught by Judo. By applying seiryoku zenyo to all of these aims, we will achieve progress and efficiency in everything." - Kano Sensei

Figure 30: This simple shift sets up a plethora of deadly techniques that Master Luiz can perform at will. It starts however, because he was super sensitive and connected to my movements. The moment he felt me push into him is when Master Luiz performed the hip shift. Now his options are endless! That's what perfect connection and sensitivity will do!

CHAPTER

12

THE GREATEST LESSON

THE GREATEST LESSON you can gain in Jiu Jitsu is this: Keep showing up. That's it. Consistent and *intelligent* practice will eventually yield great results. This has to be applied to all parts of life. If you want more wealth, more love, more passion, more skills, more of ANYTHING, you have to keep showing up no matter what.

Unless you are a super champ that never loses on the mat, you will go through spells where you lose, or get injured, or can't do what you want with your opponent. Do you give up then if you lose to a white belt? Do you give up because you can't win your division? The answer, of course, is no. In fact, it's a giant HELL NO! You have to keep showing up to practice after these episodes.

What does showing up entail? It means you keep your intentions flowing and keep consistent effort in your dreams. This is the only true magic bullet. It's magic because, over time, the small drops you add to your bucket of life will eventually pour over. If you give up after a couple weeks or months, you become a one hit wonder at best.

You have to believe in the Law of Compounding. This isn't the <u>Law of Attraction</u>, or <u>The Secret</u>, that became so popular. (I think that those aforementioned topics are rooted in the basic science of the Law of Compounding, but I'm not going to get into that here.) The Law of Compounding is simple: If you keep consistently working and adding value to the thing you are focused on, you will slowly but surely gain some commensurate positive outgrowth in that area. It simply happens.

Take money for instance. Unless you are extremely lucky and hit something huge like the Lotto or gambling, you simply don't have the odds in your favor for attaining great wealth overnight. The closest thing would be to invest in a suitable business, real estate, or stock. Even then though, you have to be relentless in your consistent effort and attention to make the endeavor more successful. It's usually invisible, but the Law of Compounding takes place all the whole time. At some point, there will be a tipping point, and then the glory will surface.

The easiest way to see this is in stocks. I love investing in stocks whether it's my IRA Roth account or personal individual stocks. In the past, I set aside a certain dollar amount each month that no matter what would be invested. Sometimes it was paltry. At other times, it was a little better. Each month, my dollar amount rose so slow it was worse than watching paint dry. However, I knew that I was never wavering in my effort to invest. Sometimes it was only

$11! It took almost 15 years of snail-like movement to happen, but when it did, my life was NEVER the same.

That feeling of attaining your dream is like achieving your Black Belt. Suddenly, the Glory, the Pleasure, the Power and Recognition of all your work and effort reveal themselves. When people see the results of successful people, they usually do not see the years of consistent hard and grinding work that those people have performed. However, there is no other way. Nothing will ever replace the daily grind of consistent hard work.

CONCLUSION

A LONG TIME AGO, before I was practicing Brazilian Jiu Jitsu and just doing Japanese and Chinese martial arts, I came across a book called, <u>Way of the Warrior</u> (formerly titled <u>The Fighting Arts</u> in the U.K.). In it, there was an interview with a true wizened master named Risuke Otake Sensei. He was the leader of an ancient traditional school of Bujitsu called Katori Shinto Ryu in Japan. The interviewer asked him about Miyamoto Musashi, one of the most famous and skilled swordsmen in the world. He is quoted all the time by martial artists, and he left behind a seminal work called <u>The Book of Five Rings</u>. As I read the interview, I was expecting Otake Sensei to say something about the fighting prowess of Musashi Sensei. Otake Sensei did, of course, give respect and consideration to Musashi's skills as a swordsman and warrior. But Otake Sensei did not feel that his training was complete. Otake Sensei felt that Musashi did not fulfill his highest sense of humanity because he did not marry, did not have kids, and basically died a hermit, dirty and unkempt.

Now there are several ways to interpret this. I personally think that Otake Sensei was trying to promote the idea that your martial arts should deeply inform and guide your life in all aspects, not just the physical. It should deepen and enhance all of your mundane and non martial-arts oriented parts of your life.

In this sense, Otake Sensei was presenting a view similar to Inner Jiu Jitsu. Of course, he was not the only one to present this idea. This idea is as old as martial arts themselves. Kano Sensei, Funakoshi Sensei, O'Sensei, Bruce Lee, and many of the Gracies and Machado brothers have all said this in one form or another. However, it is a notion that needs to be repeated over and over again.

We must integrate all aspects of life with martial arts. Otherwise, we will always be an incomplete martial artist. If we don't do this, and our training doesn't help our lives, think of all the areas that might suffer! Our marriages, our kids, our finances, our emotions, or our sense of purpose in life might be weak. Who wants to be a temporary champion on the mat but lose out on our humanity? We should seek to become the total warrior instead and enjoy our humanity to the fullest. One of the ways is to take some pro-active steps and start living life on the terms we want.

The bottom line of this book is that with your mind, your dedication, and willingness to practice, you can seriously accomplish things you didn't think possible. That's the lesson you learn in Jiu Jitsu as well. When you show up to practice consistently, work hard, the results are you get better at your game. The obstacles become less difficult to deal with, your brain adapts better to various opponents, and you start to chain your attacks more while defending wisely. Why should life be any different?

You need to consistently show up in life. It can't be a mindless attendance either. If you want results, you have to be an excellent student and demonstrate key attributes of studentship. (Master Rigan and I will explain this in the following interview.) It's essentially a non-dualistic interconnected universe where your actions affect everything, so never take your mindset and subsequent actions lightly. This is where all the great change happens.

Finally, what happens in Jiu-Jitsu, happens in life. Train accordingly.

INTERVIEW WITH LEGENDARY MASTER RIGAN MACHADO

THIS INTERVIEW WITH Legendary Master Rigan Machado was conducted in April of 2016 in preparation for this book. It was the night after the submission only tournament Fight to Win IV. Master Rigan was in attendance for the tournament watching and cheering for one of his black belts, Nobu Yagai. Professor Rigan Machado graciously blessed me with this interview and answered my questions right before he gave a great seminar for the Way of Jiu Jitsu Academy in Denver, Colorado.

Author: At what point in your personal training did Jiu Jitsu become more than just a physical art?

Rigan: *There was not just one moment, there was a variety of moments which helped me a lot. I had a few amazing coaches: Rolls Gracie, Carlson Gracie, Carlos Gracie Jr... These different coaches brought me something unique. I'll* *give you an example in regards to Rolls Gracie. What I loved about Rolls Gracie was he was pure action. He was a guy who believed in not just thinking something or talking about something without doing it. He was a man who put into action everything he said he would do. I remember one time we had a workout in the morning with a big athlete named "Ronaldo". He was not just a Jiu Jitsu athlete, but a big body builder and the strongest person in our academy. I remember one time he mentioned he went and trained in Judo at another academy. He came back and bragged about how he threw and submitted all the players at this Judo academy, including the national champion. This man said that because he submitted everyone including the national champion, that he didn't think Judo was any good. Rolls didn't say anything, he just listened to this man brag. The next day, Rolls said, "Today, we start the training standing. Ronaldo, you are going to be my partner." Rolls proceeded to throw Ronaldo twenty times on the ground. After this, Rolls said, "Now, we start standing and we finish the fight on the ground." Rolls then would start the match with a throw and then submit Ronaldo on the ground. After he did this numerous times, Rolls explained, "We **never badmouth someone or something if it can be good for us. We use anything that can be positive for our benefit**."*

This was a great lesson I learned from Rolls Gracie. He was a guy who didn't talk much but lived a life of action. Basically, you should use everything to your advantage. It happens all the time in life and in training. People come from all over to learn and to teach. People have so many skills with so many aspects of life. In the end, you have to look at the results that people make. The actions will speak louder than words. That's what I love about Jiu Jitsu and its application in life. If you have great actions in training, it will have a great effect on the mat. If you have great actions in life, you will have a great life as well.

Author: So it sounds like being open minded to everything?

Rigan: *Yes. It's not about dreaming or talking, it's about action in life. Make something happen. That's what I learned at the academy and that's what I try to bring to people now.*

Author: Next question. How do you teach Jiu Jitsu to students for success in life? Do you have specific ways to use Jiu Jitsu as a way of life?

Rigan: *Jiu Jitsu is a platform of experiences I have for my life. I have had many different teachers and they have all given me different experiences. I feel lucky that I have been part of this big history from the beginning of this sport in Brazil to today. I have seen many steps. But one of the things I try to give to my students is this: It's very easy to show techniques. The most important thing is to teach a student how to become a better person. That's when I believe you become a good teacher. If you are just interested in techniques, you can go to YouTube or see someone in a seminar and learn this thing and that thing. But it's not just about teaching new techniques, it's about teaching the philosophy of how to apply Jiu Jitsu for your own life and how to help other people in their life as well.*

Author: Right on! I know Professor Nobu fought Baret Yoshida...

Rigan: *It was a good fight.*

Author: It was a good fight, and that guy is a legend. The cool thing I remember at the beginning of the fight in the introduction was that Professor Nobu was saying this was a spiritual thing for him to fight. I totally relate to that and what you're saying as well. That's what this book is about.

Rigan: *Yes.*

Author: I have two more questions. You're becoming very famous now. I see you have tons of celebrity students; Keanu Reeves, Ashton Kutcher, and now Tai Lopez...

Rigan (smiling): *Tai Lopez is a good guy.*

Author: I admire him and I admire his work!

Rigan: *You need to come to Beverly Hills and hang out.*

Author (both of us laughing): I hope! I foresee that happening in the future! So what is it that you offer? I mean these guys are coming to you, seeking you out, you are attracting these guys . . .

Rigan: *I have a story for you but I cannot mention the name. Celebrities are like me and you, they are human. But they are different. They have this super popularity around them. Fame. They have this amazing power, and by power I mean, they can endorse something and the next day it can be a big product. They have this big image. And some celebrities can have the problem of getting affected here (Rigan points to his temples). They get this ego, and every fan blows that ego up like a big balloon.*

I remember this one celebrity. He is a famous musician. I can't mention his name but he came in one day with his entourage and bodyguard. They just came in, walked right by me, had their shoes on the mat, went into the locker room, and came out and started to warm up. They were talking and had no idea about what the etiquette of the academy was. The academy is like a temple. We have a model, honor, and order of things we embrace as a martial artist. I went up to him and said, "Sir, can I talk to you?" He said, "Sure." I said, "I need to know what is the procedure for teaching you." He said, "Just treat me like any other person." I said, "OK, good. This is how it's going to go then. In order for you to get the best version of me as an instructor, I need you to be the best version of you as a student. When you come in, you have to stop and talk to me. You have to ask permission to come on the mat. I cannot have any interruptions from your entourage talking. I understand you have a bodyguard because you're famous, but the bodyguard needs to wait outside. You are here to be a student, and in order for that to happen, I need to be your teacher and act like that and you need to act like an appropriate student. I spent 40 years of my life to get the respect that my belt holds and to be able to teach you now. My students call me 'sir'. And in this world, because you're beginning, you have to call me 'sir'. That's the way we have respect for coach and student. And the moment we have this understanding, we're going to have good work. But if you talk in class, walk by me without asking permission, there will not be respect. Without that, there will be no relationship."

That's the way I build up my celebrity students. I bring them back to reality. When you come to my academy, you're the student, I'm the coach, you listen to me. You understand? This works in many different ways. When you start to train a celebrity, you have to treat them like everybody else. You make a mistake, I'm going to call you on it. You make them do it again. When you train like this, you build up the best person from the inside out. This kind of training is amazing because a lot of these celebrities struggle with problems like smoking or weight control. Jiu Jitsu brings them back. It demonstrates humbleness and discipline, which they sometimes need. They start to realize, 'Wait a minute, I'm a person before I'm a celebrity. I'm not better than anyone else.' Some celebrities miss that. They miss being treated like a human being. I got better at doing this. You have to be very sensitive in this. Training a celebrity is sometimes like training a fighter. They both have had their egos blown up like a big balloon for a long time. You cannot just explode that balloon all at once. You just let some of that air out, little by little until they are normal and then you can start to train. It's a process that I believe you can develop. Once one celebrity has this experience, they tell another celebrity, and then another with a recommendation. I've built up this reputation now.

A lot of these celebrities are awesome guys. It's an amazing thing, getting to know these guys. Some of them are amazing people.

Author: I can see why now celebrities are attracted to you. You empower them and bring them down back to humbleness. They feel human around you. Well, thank you. Thank you for endorsing this project!

Rigan: *Good luck with this project.*

Author: This project was inspired by you in a way. I remember long ago, looking at your website, and you had something on it that said, Jiu Jitsu for Life. I thought to myself that this is it! This is what Jiu Jitsu should be used for. Not just for the obvious physical benefit it would give, but also applying the principles to help with marriage, financial success, getting along with bosses and regular relationships. I appreciate your help in this. Thank you!

LESSONS GLEANED FROM THE INTERVIEW WITH MASTER RIGAN
(The mat is a microcosm of the Universe)

THIS CONCLUDED OUR interview. We talked briefly about Professor Rigan's black belt Nobu Yagai's match the night before with Baret Yoshida and I shook his hand and wrapped this whole thing up. As I write down these words and contemplate on some of what Master Rigan said about the lesson Rolls taught him, it hits me like a ton of bricks. Words are just words, actions are so much stronger. **Actions** are the defining characteristics that determine success or failure. We need massive action to get where we want to. I hope this book helps people see Jiu Jitsu as a strategic plan to implement action steps towards whatever it is they want in life.

When Master Rigan discussed that everyone that comes into the academy has to follow the rules and become the best student they can be so the instructor can be the best instructor he can be, it reminded me of some fantastic spiritual thinking. In the 3rd line of the *Pratyabhijna Hrdayam* (Heart of Recognition scripture) from Kashmir Shaivism, it basically states that the universe is set up in a system of reciprocal relationships. In essence, in order for you to get the best response from the universe, you have to give the best version of yourself to the universe. It's a simple teaching that can be substantiated to a degree from basic quantum mechanics. It goes like this: If you want to have a great partner in life, you have to become a great partner yourself to attract that partner. Your mindset has a great bearing on the reality you observe, and that observation becomes altered by your mindset. That's what the Observer Effect[13] of quantum mechanics is all about. Nothing is truly objective in the sense that it is detached from the subject. YOU ARE THE SUBJECT, therefore you influence the object by the mere fact of observing! You are a co-creator of the universe, a participant in the reality you make! If you take the opposite mindset that the universe is out there, and random forces will ultimately sway and control you, then guess what: you will reap the fruits of someone who believes in that narrative. You will believe and respond to a universe where random and uncontrollable forces ultimately control and dominate your life. You can imagine the concluding emotional and mental state of such a person.

The Jiu Jitsu academy is a microcosm of the universe. The teacher represents potential open situations in life. If you are a crappy disrespectful student, you will have a crappy relationship with the teacher and the whole system will crumble. Conversely, if you act from your highest sense, then the teacher (assuming the teacher is

---

13   The idea in quantum mechanics that it is possible for the subject to have an effect on the object observed. See http://www.fredalanwolf.com/

also operating from his highest sense of self) will give you his best, and the relationship will yield the greatest and most positive results. This goes for all relationships. It's not just relationships with people, however. All of life is a relationship. There's relationship of self with our thoughts and various mutations of relationship with nature or our environment. There is no escaping relating with the world. Since this is so, you might as well make your relationships serve you in the best way possible. Choose the best thoughts, and become the best version of yourself you can be so the universe responds accordingly!

DEDICATIONS

T O BE IN the company of great friends is to have a fulfilled life. I could not have done this project without the friendship and help of certain key people.

This book is dedicated first and foremost to Master Rigan Machado, who I consider an incredible man. He is one of the foremost ambassadors to his family's art of Brazilian Jiu Jitsu. I will be forever grateful for his teachings and blessings on this project.

Minh Bui is one of the country's most prolific Jiu Jitsu photographers and he was the photographer for this book. Contact him for any of your photography needs or to order some pics of your favorite Jiu Jitsu artists: minhbui@gmail.com

Kit Hedman did the cover of this book and several others. His amazing work can be seen at http://kithedmanphotography.blogspot.com/ and you can contact him at hedmanphoto@aol.com

My instructors and training partners from the past and present at Way of Jiu Jitsu and Sanctuary BJJ have been instrumental in my growth on the physical path of Jiu Jitsu. I thank you all for all our years together (especially Professor Dave for starting me on the physical path!) Special shout out to Fight to Win competitor Nobu Yagai and Naga champion Matt Cram as well as Judo Olympian athlete Charlee

Minkin and Jiu Jitsu World League champion Ben Lowry for being Jiu Jitsu models. Check out wayofjiujitsu.com and sanctuarybjj.com for some of the best Jiu Jitsu in the Denver area. While you're here in Denver, you should check out the incredible denverbjjseminars.com of Ray Castillo, as he is always bringing the greatest Jiu Jitsu athletes from around the world to Denver. It's completely open to all schools!

To all my teachers and professors through the years too numerous to list. Those that taught me the Dharma of Lord Buddha directly, or indirectly from my secular but equally wise teachers, I thank you all!

For my teachers in Kashmir Shaivism, Hinduism, Hatha Yoga, and meditation, I will forever be grateful. Big shout out to Chris Wallis for his friendship. He's an amazing teacher: www.tantrikstudies.org

To all those wonderful positive psychology teachers I have had the pleasure to actually learn from, you embody the spiritual teachings in a way that is secular and meaningful. Thank you!

My dear friend and actualizer of human potential, Barry Napier, owner of PR Fitness and Life Change Technologies, thank you for believing in this project. Without you, it would not have achieved the level of success it did! coachbarry@theprdiet.com

My greatest teacher and friend that I have is my wife. Ignacia, you have been my catalyst for learning and using these techniques. Thank you, I love you, and I dedicate this to you and our family!

CITATIONS

Bryon, Thomas. Dhammapada: The Sayings of the Buddha. New York: Shambhala Publications, 1993.

Chodron, Pema. The Wisdom of No Escape and the Path of Loving-Kindness. Boston: Shambhala Publications, 2001.

Kano, Jigoro. Mind over Muscle: Writings from the Founder of Judo. Trans. Nancy H. Ross. New York: Kodansha, 2005.

BJJ Training Journal.(2014) Version 1.6 Mobile Application Software. Retrieved by https://itunes.apple.com/us/app/bjj-training-journ...

Reid, Howard; Croucher, Michael. The Way of the Warrior. New York: Overlook Press, 1984.

Shantananda, Swami. The Splendor of Recognition: An Exploration of the Pratyabhijna Hrdayam, a Text on the Ancient Science of the Soul. New York: Siddha Yoga Publications, 2003.

Trungpa, Chogyam. Training the Mind and Cultivating Loving Kindness. Boston: Shambhala Publications, 1993.

Made in United States
Troutdale, OR
11/13/2023

14546874R10096